REA

ACPL ITEM
3 1833 04914 4055
DISCARDED

Learning
the Language
of Babylon

Extreme Teen Edition

D1516325

Terry M. Crist

PRESS

SEP 2 2 2005

Copyright © 2004 by Terry M. Crist

Learning the Language of Babylon – Extreme Teen Edition
by Terry M. Crist

Printed in the United States of America

Library of Congress Control Number: 2004097409

ISBN 1-594678-09-X

All rights reserved solely by the author. The author guarantees all contents are original and do not infringe upon the legal rights of any other person or work. This book or parts thereof may not be reproduced in any form, stored in a retrieval system or transmitted in any form by any means—electronic, mechanical, photocopy, recording or otherwise—without prior written permission of the author, except as provided by United States of America copyright law. The views expressed in this book are not necessarily those of the publisher.

Unless otherwise noted, all Scripture quotations are from the New King James Version of the Bible. Copyright © 1979, 1980, 1982 by Thomas Nelson, Inc., publishers. Used by permission.

Scripture quotations marked "NIV" are from the Holy Bible, New International Version. Copyright © 1973, 1978, 1984, International Bible Society. Used by permission.

Cover design by Bridget Jentzsch

www.xulonpress.com

What Leaders Are Saying About This Book!

Unbelievers do not speak Christianese. Speaking Christianese to an unbeliever is like speaking Swahili to a German. This book shows Christians how to speak lovingly and relationally to the world around us.

Dr. Tony Evans, Founder,
The Urban Alternative, Senior Pastor,
Oak Cliff Bible Fellowship, Dallas, Texas

A map for the road back to becoming relevant as a Christian, *Learning the Language of Babylon, Extreme Teen Edition* is not an option if we are to make disciples of all nations. Terry Crist is one of a new generation of revolutionaries sounding a clear trumpet preparing the Church for battle.

Rice Broocks
Senior Pastor, Bethel Chapel, Nashville, Tennessee
President, Morning Star International

In *Learning the Language of Babylon*, Terry Crist boldly conveys the direction that the Holy Spirit has set for the Church. As a student of societal trends and culture, he warns the Christian not to retreat from the battle of ideas by closing off access to the marketplace. Terry skillfully teaches the reader how to understand and speak the language of Babylon – the postmodern culture in which we live – from a transformational perspective. This book is a survival guide for the twenty-first century Christian and a must-read!

David Ireland
Senior Pastor, Christ Church, Montclair, New Jersey
Author, *Failure is Written in Pencil*

Terry Crist has always been a man ahead of his time. His insights and wisdom have influenced people for many years. Once again, Terry comes through. This book is sure to take you to new levels in God.

Tim Storey
Author, Motivational Speaker, Hollywood, California

Foreword

In my travels, many pastors, youth group leaders, parents and students ask me to share with them what I feel to be some of the most effective ways of impacting our culture. My first thought usually is that when I (by His grace), stop trying to change the people around me, and change myself by turning towards God's Kingdom, listening to His voice, and obeying it as a sacrifice unto Him, the strangest thing happens...God begins to use the changes in me to effect others.

But there are many thoughts and writings on this subject. Some (to one extreme) seem so concerned with being relevant, they grasp at each oncoming trend until they finally either run out of breath or lose their footing rendering themselves irrelevant. Others seem so caught up on polishing the outside of a cup, they send most away thirsty.

Pastor Terry Crist's *Learning the Language of Babylon, Extreme Teen Edition,* does what many have failed to achieve. It reveals that our greatest barriers to evangelism are not theological or philosophical, but cultural. It confirms in me that there is more of God's kingdom on earth than sitting on top of the roof of my house, bags packed, throwing rocks at anyone I see fit, while I'm waiting for Jesus to come back. It leads to the path, that if we walk, we will be pleasantly surprised to hear the rustlings of many we come in contact with, asking us the way.

Let this book help us to do away with the Morse code we have created ourselves, come down of our rooftops, open our font doors and pull the string on those "graceless" curtains of 'us versus them'.

Let it be a reminder to all disciples of Christ that we weren't put here to form a sub-culture with its own t-shirts, bumper stickers, industries and rock stars. Let it show us, whether at work, around the dinner table, in shopping malls or congress halls, to make a difference, we must live the difference! And finally, let it give us cups full of living water with the proper tongues to call the thirsty to drink.

I pray these writings change your life as they have mine.

Peter Furler, The Newsboys

Read this first!

There has never been a generation quite like this one in the history of the world. You have been blessed with the best and the worst that mankind has to offer. You've inherited everything good that previous generations have sacrificed to discover, from technology to medicine. But you've also received a legacy of brokenness, and frustration, which is the result of man's recognition that he cannot solve the greatest human dilemma of all, the problem of evil in the world. Just beneath the thin veneer of modern sophistication there runs a thread of desperation. If we can't fix what's really broken, what next?

Learning the Language of Babylon was written to accomplish two goals. First, I want you to understand who you are. It's Christ in you, the hope of glory in this broken world. Second, I want to equip you to fulfill your God given assignment in this generation. I want to see you armed and dangerous.

This *50 Day Spiritual Advance* is meant to be absorbed one day at a time. Only by carefully reading and prayerfully considering the message can you arise to the challenge of changing the world by engaging the culture.

Each day of this spiritual advance has four basic components: a thought provoking message, a section designed to help you strengthen your heart, another segment to help you sharpen your mind, and a truth to be acted upon. So read this carefully and become all you were created to be!

Terry Crist

P.S. After reading this book, drop me a line and let me know how your life has been touched.

ðay 1

Diary of a Cultural Captive

Dateline 605 B.C.
Journal Entry

I'll never forget that summer. The heat was unbearable—you know the kind, where all you wanna do is stay cool and try not to move. Of course, trying to remain still and cool really was not an option for most of us. Our circumstances kept us on the move, stumbling along under the burning heat of the midday sun. But the physical pain could not compare to the ache of knowing that everything I loved was gone, forever.

I wanted to pinch myself, as if I could actually wake up from this horrible nightmare. But I couldn't. It wasn't a dream. It wasn't a delusion. It was a reality of the worst kind. Twenty-four hours earlier my greatest challenge was to find something interesting to keep me occupied through the summer vacation; now I was fighting for my life.

The attack caught us by surprise. The village, that evening, was filled with the usual sights, sounds, and delicious smells as the women diligently worked to prepare the evening meal. Our men had just returned from the fields and were busy finishing their chores before nightfall. The sentries were inattentive, joking with one another as they released the stress of another boring day. And then the "hordes of hades" broke forth upon us.

The barbarians had planned their attack well and left no escape route open. If I hadn't returned to the field that evening to retrieve the sickle forgotten by my younger brother, I might not be alive today. When the dawn broke the following morning I could see that our homes had been burned, our village destroyed and the sacred Temple reduced to rubble. But those things could be replaced. The dead couldn't be.

As a matter of fact, lots of people were dead—mostly men—

murdered in cold blood. I will never forget the horrible images of the blood of my people drying in the dust of Jerusalem. When the final resister was killed, the remaining women were beaten and their children taken from them.

The survivors were chained together like a pack of dogs and led away to Babylon. I remember the eerie feeling that swept over me as I looked around. People who were once proud and strong now hung their heads in shame. It was all I could do to keep from screaming aloud, "God, where are You now that we need You most?"

Why had God allowed this to happen? Of course, I guess we should have seen it coming. In a way, it was our own fault. I was only a teenager at the time, but even I was smart enough to know that the way things had become could only lead to trouble.

Israel was a strong, proud, and united nation at one time, but my ancestors had allowed the nation to be ripped apart and divided into two separate nations—Judah and Israel. Looking back, it's easy to see how each nation was guilty of sin. We had disregarded God's law and turned a deaf ear to His prophets. And to think that—despite our sinful way of life—we thought that Jerusalem was this "impenetrable fortress" because it was built high on a hill. A lot of good that did us. Our villages were destroyed, homes burned, and survivors taken as slaves. We would never again see our homeland or worship in the holy city. But the greatest battle was yet to come. Within days we would be thrown into a culture that ridiculed our faith and oppressed our worship.

I wish I could say that there was a happy ending to all of this gloom and doom, but I can't. It's been many years since that unforgettable summer and I still haven't seen the salvation of Israel. I guess that's why our people call it faith—desperately clinging to hope, irrationally testifying to what has not yet come to pass. My prayer is that God will one day deliver His people and bring victory to Israel. No human being, especially a child of God, should be forced to endure this kind of slavery. Not me. And certainly not you.

'Til next time,

Daniel

Reforming Your Heart

Read Deuteronomy 31:6.

Have you ever wondered if God had forgotten about you or left you alone to try to handle a problem by yourself?

Looking back on that situation, do you still believe that God had abandoned you?

There's an old proverb that says, "Hindsight is 20/20." What does this mean? Have you ever found yourself wondering why you weren't "smart enough" to realize that you were headed for trouble—until it was too late?

Reforming Your Mind

Reflect: *God is always trying to get our attention. What are the warning signs from God that you feel you have been ignoring?*

Relate: *Right now, I personally am struggling with...*

Reforming Your Actions

Spend at least thirty minutes in prayer, asking God to open your eyes to the spiritual reality around you. Pray that He will give you wisdom and understanding as you continue on this *50-Day Spiritual Advance.*

ðay 2

Babylon Smackdown

The battle between Judah and Babylon may have begun thousands of years ago, but it is still going strong even today. How is that possible? Simple. These two spiritual/political powers are like the ultimate WWF Divas. Talk about your no-holds-barred grudge match—picture this

> *"Ladies and gentleman, welcome to the fight of all time, the war to end all wars, the Battle Divine! This one is for the heavyweight championship of the universe!*
>
> *"Crouching in the left corner, wearing all black (and what a body—ooh-la-la), smokin' hot, representing the legions of hell and the passions of men—Babylon the Great!*
>
> *"Standing tall in the right corner and wearing white, smooth and cool, representing the throngs of heaven and the passion of God, the beautiful Bride of Christ, the victorious warrior princess—Judah, the Hope of Zion!"*

You think that sounds too strange to be true? Take a look around, for crying out loud. The spirit of Babylon has infected Christianity like a venereal disease: false doctrines, immoral living, liberal theology, spiritual tolerance, and moral relativism (to name a few). In the name of spiritual tolerance, truth is compromised in order to have an inoffensive Christianity—a form of godliness, but denying the pure power of the Gospel.

Let's face it. Even in your lifetime American culture has continued to change dramatically. While we were looking the other way, playing church and making out with the world, the culture rotted away and we were unprepared for the results. *How and why did we let this happen?*

There was a time, believe it or not, when the majority of people agreed upon right and wrong. But this ain't Kansas anymore, Toto. Babylon the witch is ruling the roost and we've rolled over to let her scratch our bellies. We have traded our collective conscience, our sense of right and wrong, for freedom from restraint. Prior to post-modernism, most individuals asked themselves, *Is this the right thing to do?* Now, almost every student entering the university believes, or says he believes, that truth is relative.

That's really sad. No, I changed my mind. It's worse. It's disgusting.

We desperately need a wake-up call.

God's purpose and plan for his bride is truly out-of-this world, for both now and eternity. But living in the holy city means that we must be willing to engage in the battle. The Jerusalem-Babylon battle continues in every nation in every generation, transcending time, space, geography, and race. This conflict is about preserving the remnants of righteousness in our UB (University of Babylon) society while also taking back the ground lost in previous conflicts. You have been destined by God to help make this happen. He wants to use your head, your heart, and your hands. Are you ready to rumble?

Reforming Your Heart

Religious tolerance seems to be the new "virtue" of the day. Anyone who says another person's religious beliefs are wrong is accused of being a bigot. But look at 1 Peter 2:7–8.

How can we have a Christianity that is tolerant and inoffensive if Jesus Himself was called the rock that makes men fall?

Is there a difference between offensive Christianity and offensive Christians? Explain.

Reforming Your Mind

Reflect: *Do you feel there may be areas in your life where you compromised your ethics or standards in order to be accepted by those around you?*

Relate: *I know that _____ is the right thing to do, but I struggle with staying true to those convictions.*

Reforming Your Actions

Pray this prayer:

Search me, O God, and know my heart; test me and know my anxious thoughts. See if there is any offensive way in me, and lead me in the way everlasting (Psalm 139:23-24.)

Now spend time allowing God to speak to you. Repent and commit to going forward in Him.

Ðay 3

You've Been Punked

Toward the end of the nineteenth century, the Christianity in America was faced with a number of ideas that radically opposed the Bible. For the first time in modern history the world was no longer viewed and understood in supernatural ways. Many people began to consider God "dead", if He ever were even existent to begin with. Modern man had figured the world out, and God obviously had nothing to do with it. These ideas laid siege to the North American Church just as surely as Nebuchadnezzar surrounded Jerusalem to destroy it. The battle lines were blurred, the face of the enemy obscured, and our objective not clearly identified. This battlefield became "the most fundamental controversy to wrack the churches since the Reformation."[1] As a result, the Church split up—left and right.

Going left were those who buckled under the pressure of these new ideas rather than engage in a battle over them. They made peace with the enemies by giving up their most basic beliefs (biblical creationism, the sinfulness of man, the virgin birth, inerrancy of scripture). Rather than engage in a battle over truth, they settled for a couple of really bad ideas. First, God was now "the big guy upstairs," always ready to overlook sin and offer some free love. Second, it was believed that the university of Babylon (identified from this point on as the one and only "UB") society could be reformed without the Word of God. Besides, it really was much easier this way.

Uh, yeah. Sure...

Headed right was those who were theologically conservative (i.e., they still believed the basic teachings of the Bible) yet out of touch. They remained faithful to the Word of God and the fundamentals of the faith (hence the term *fundamentalists*). But, they abandoned all hope of cultural influence. Rather than engage in the battle of ideas, they retreated from the mainstream of culture into a holy huddle. Some fundamentalist extremists even adopted a theology of anti-intellectualism, refusing to learn about anything for fear of having their theology challenged.

Respected historian Arnold Toynbee once studied 21 civilizations and discovered five characteristics common to rotting "Babylonian" cultures. Every society he examined shared in a common crisis. They seemed to lack a sense of stability, believing that life was meaningless and out of control. As a result they succumbed to escapism or social negligence, retreating into entertainment and recreation. Tolerance rendered them powerless to transform the social decline. Yielding to their unrestrained appetites, they abandoned moral absolutes and embraced wholesale promiscuity. These disintegrating societies contended with a continual sense of guilt and self-hated. Most were destroyed by internal culture wars—just like the ones that we have been experiencing in America.[2]

I know, I know, it seems ridiculous. After all, who in their right minds would believe both creation *and* evolution? Who would believe that sex outside of marriage is sin but heavy "making out" is not. What kind of pea brain would believe that God's word was actually written by men and therefore, is bound to have errors in it (minor ones, of course)? Oops, sorry about that. I forgot—*we* are the pea brains who have swallowed these lies—hook, line, and sinker.

The battle for the nations of the earth, I am convinced, will ultimately be a struggle for control of the culture—who is in charge and who will set the UB social agenda. Nothing short of a great civil war of values rages throughout North America; it is a war over ideas. The definitive question facing the Church of the twenty-first century is this: *Who is in charge—God or man?*

Reforming Your Heart

Read James 2:14, 18.

Be honest with yourself: Are there some areas in your life where you have attempted to divorce your faith and your way of living? In other words, have you adopted any hypocritical ways that allow you to believe one way and yet live in contradiction to that belief?

Reforming Your Mind

Reflect: *Do you believe that the Bible is 100% true and accurate? Why or why not?*

Relate: *(1) I sometimes struggle with believing that _____.*
(2) I sometimes struggle with making myself obey the biblical command to _____ .

Reforming Your Actions

Read Joshua 24:14-15.

Make a decision today. Recognize that this decision may mean your life and your soul—choose wisely.

ðay 4

Bound by Our Own Beliefs

America has been invaded by demonic forces that enslave the mind and spirit. Sounds a little hard to believe, I know. It's because demons are not—contrary to popular Christian opinion—ignorant. They're ancient, angelic beings. They've been watching the human race for thousands of years. And they've figured out that if they hide "within" the culture, they can easily target the current generation. Their aim is to invade, enslave, and employ you and your friends in the kingdom of darkness.

So what do you think? Take a look around you, Toto; we aren't any closer to Kansas than we were a few pages ago. Is it working? Or does the Kingdom of God rule and reign on your campus? That one should be easy!

Like many other Christians, I was raised believing that God's plan to redeem mankind was limited to a few determined Christians who resisted all forms of worldliness and remained "free from spiritual defilement" until the end of the age. We were convinced that the anti-Christ would suck up most believers and only a pure remnant of enduring Christians would barely resist. Our greatest hope was to be evacuated miraculously from this God-forsaken world just hours before the powers of darkness closed in for the deathblow.

Sure, we believed that Jesus' death on the cross was the greatest act in all of human history. Yes, we saw it as the triumph of life conquering death, the Son of God removing the curse from the sons of men. But even so, our primary goal in life was to be rescued from this demonized generation. We had developed a "remnant theology" to protect us from our pain.

I mean, let's be honest. My generation lacked (and many *still* lack) the faith to believe that anything positive could happen on this darkened planet. We were pretty sure that there was nothing we could do about it by ourselves. We had allowed God to be ruled out of the equation. Yep, things looked pretty hopeless.

As the Church retreated from the public arena, the spirit of Babylon gained a foothold in contemporary culture and began to turn everything upside down. Righteousness became bigotry and intolerance. The Church became, in the infamous words of soldier-turned-wrestler-turned politician Jessie Ventura, "a crutch for the weak." And so was born the Christian ghetto, a fringe element, a subculture within the greater culture. The values we once held dear slowly disintegrated before our eyes.

As the culture deteriorated, we Christians focused our attention on other things, inward things. We stopped planning for the future and began focusing on our escape. Rapture fever swept through the Church like a raging fever trying to burn out the infection of our pain and confusion. The desire to reform "Babylonian" society was replaced by the longing to escape the pain of watching our culture worsen. We slowly began to accept our exile as permanent.

Reforming Your Heart

Read Ephesians 6:10-17.

It's easy to read a passage of scripture such as this and dismiss it, After all, most of us have never even seen a devil, right? Even if he is real, he isn't after you, right? He was after the true heroes of faith, like Jesus, Peter, and Paul.

Of course. That's silly. Why would the devil be after you? What threat are you to him?

Reforming Your Mind

Reflect: *As a follower of Christ, what precautions are you taking each day to protect yourself against the attacks of our enemy, the devil?*

Relate: *I'll have to be honest—it is easier to retreat than advance. Here are some ways that I have failed to make a difference in my world...*

Reforming Your Actions

Make a list of three ways you've "stuck your head in the cultural sand" instead of engaging in the battle over right and wrong. Now spend some time asking the Lord to forgive you and empower you to change that pattern!

ðay 5

The Recruit

Growing up as a PK (preacher's kid), I loved hearing the stories of Daniel. Daniel put the "oo" in smooth. He was like the 007 of the Old Testament: extremely confident, good looking, strong-willed, and able to get out of predicaments that even Bond himself might have trouble with. When the king offered Daniel steak and lobster, Daniel refused and lived off rabbit food. And he still came out stronger, healthier, and better looking than the king's puppets! He even decoded the cryptic message left by the ghostly hand that wrote all over the king's walls. *But somehow, I never saw Daniel's life as an example of how to reclaim the cultural terrain from the hand of the enemy!*

Daniel was a nothing short of remarkable. As a matter of fact, the story is even better when you realize that Daniel was a teenager! That's right, a real-life high school stud. But more important, Daniel was a man of God, 110% authentic! And somehow, he managed to sort out the challenge of demonstrating his faith in a hostile culture. So how'd he do it? Well if you must know, I'll tell you what I believe was the secret to his success. Move your face a little closer to the book because I need to whisper it:

> *He was willing to learn the* language *of Babylon without being nourished by the* spirit *of Babylon.*

That's it. And in so doing, he established an easy to follow pattern for me, you, and anyone else attempting to serve as missionaries to a "foreign" culture. Sort of an evangelistic dot-to-dot.

So here's the deal: We will never make a difference in this world unless we are willing to learn its language. We must "sing our song in the land of Babylon." This means that we have to be a little…well, vulnerable. No more hiding in our holy huddles and only going to Christian malls and drinking Christian coffee.

Now, I know what you are thinking. You're thinking, *Duh.*

So maybe adults are more likely to be the ones who have retreated and given up on making a difference. But before you get the big head, you need to ask yourself how many people you've won to Christ this year.

"Ohh, ohhhh! I can't see! I can't see! There's a plank in my eye!"

Just because you were born into this culture doesn't mean you are automatically making a difference. That's something that you—that we *all*—must learn to do, one step at a time.

Much to the chagrin (look it up, it's a great word) of your elders, things will never again be the way they were in the fifties. The only way back to cultural and spiritual Jerusalem is by a different train than the one we rode in on. Times have changed, and the good old days are gone forever. We must chart a new course. I am on a quest—a mission to rescue the lost and reclaim the culture. How about you? Wanna take a ride?

Reforming Your Heart

Daniel was bold. No doubt about it. But honestly, even though he sounds like Superboy on caffeine, he was just a normal kid who happened to be serious about his faith. How serious are you?

Read Mark 8:34–38.

Could you remain true if the government put a target on your back? Could you say no to sex and drugs if they were legalized on your campus?

Could you stand up for Christ if your school officials threatened to expel you because of your faith?

Reforming Your Mind

Reflect: *We've all blown it. Where have you compromised your faith in order to make things easier on yourself?*

Relate: *I could have a much greater impact on my friends if I would only...*

Reforming Your Actions

Don't try to do it all in one day. Baby steps, that's the plan. "Dot-to-dot." So today, find someone you know who isn't a Christian and start building a relationship. Your mission: to learn how to speak the language of spiritual Babylon.

Tip: That means listening more than talking.

ðay 6

The Framework of Captivity

We consistently hear the United States referred to as the "world's only remaining superpower." That's a pretty weird thought. If that's true (and it certainly seems to be), that sort of makes the US the dominant force in the world today. But even if that were true, it still does not compare to the power of Nebuchadnezzar. Think about it.

The US may be known as a rich and powerful country, but we don't rule the world. We rule our own country, but our citizens submit to the laws and rules of other countries whenever they are visiting. Even our military, when in other countries, respect the laws and customs of that country. But Nebuchadnezzar was different. Very different. He was the first ruler in history to *dominate* the entire known world. For you *Trekkies* out there, he was like the Borg—if he touched it, he controlled it. Resistance was *very* futile.

Since he couldn't *assimilate* (nano-tecnology hadn't quite gone public yet), this pre-tech Borg king developed a program designed to disenculturate the Jews—that is, to strip them of their identity. He isolated all of the healthy, smart young Jewish stallions and attempted to demoralize them. You know…break 'em down.

Notice several similarities between the challenges Daniel faced and our present spiritual conditions.

First, Daniel was a fired-up spiritual revolutionary sent to live in an oppressive, ungodly, sin-infested culture. You know, like Hollywood. Of course, even Hollywood's depravity can't be blamed on a "pagan Babylonian" society. Instead, we live in a post-Christian "Babylonian" society. Paganism is a pre-Christian condition. It's what you have in places that have never heard the Gospel. A post-Christian "Babylonian" society develops after the Gospel is heard and rejected. That's Hollywood. Hey, that's most of the world today.

Second, although Daniel was free to practice his religion privately, he was required to respond in a "politically correct" manner when in the presence of the Babylonians.

Of course, you and I would have trouble being able to identify with *that* (visualize strong sarcastic facial distortions of author here).

If I hear one more person try to use the "separation of church and state" mantra in order to prevent the church from being the church, I think I'm going to puke. If any one of those Babble-on-ians would actually *read* the constitution, they would be forced to admit that it doesn't support the things they try to use it to support. But that's another issue...

Third, Daniel fought his guts out to prevent the Babylonians from re-defining, labeling, and rejecting his true identity.

Can you imagine showing up for school on the first day and listening as your teacher checked the roll, only to have her change your name on the spot?

Ms. Prankard: *John Smith.*

John: *Here.*

Ms. Prankard: *John, from this moment on your name will be Ailuv Prankard.*

You get the picture. Guess that means you're going to have to change all those monogrammed sweaters. Or maybe you'd be happier with a nice bar code tattooed on your forehead?

Reforming Your Heart

Read Romans 12:2..

Where do you get your identity? What makes you who you are? What do you suppose others say about you when you aren't around? Would they describe you using the world's "pattern," or God's?

Being relevant is a good thing. But has your attempt at relevance caused you to lose your identity as a child of God?

Reforming Your Mind

Reflect: *Can you think of an example of when being "politically correct" means sacrificing your ability to be "biblically correct"?*

Relate: *I know I shouldn't, but I sometimes think that what matters most is whether or not people think I am...*

Reforming Your Actions

pend some time thinking about what it means to be conformed to God's pattern instead of the world's. Now pick one example of God's pattern and determine that you will do whatever He asks in order for that trait to become part of who you are every day.

ðay 7

What's in a Name?

Chances are, your name was given to you because:

- Your great, great grandmother Ethel, on your mom's side, had that name.
- It reminded your parents of some special place.
- Your parents thought it was "groovy."
- Your dad felt like being teased was a great character-building experience and didn't want you to miss out.

Of course, you could be one of the few whose name was specifically chosen because of its meaning, but it isn't likely. In biblical times, however, the character and destiny of a child were thought to be revealed in his or her name.

Basically, this is how it went down.

A newborn was carefully guarded and observed for seven days after birth, during which time the parents had the responsibility of discovering and defining that child's destiny.

Talk about your high-pressure experience! I can see it now, as little Dur listens while his parents explain his name.

Mom: *Well son, it means "to stack up."*

Dur: *Why would you choose a name like that? What could you possibly have been thinking?*

Dad: *Now settle down, Duh, er, uh, I mean Dur. You mother and I really had a hard time figuring out what you were going to be when you grew up. Naming a child is a very stressful responsibility.*

Dur: *But why Dur?*

Dad: *Because all you cared about was playing with your pet rocks and stacking them up. It just seemed to fit...and we were out of time.*

The rest, as they say, is history.

Each of the four young men in captivity in Babylon carried Hebrew names reflecting a portion of the character and nature of almighty God.

Daniel in Hebrew means "God's judge."

Hananiah means "beloved of the Lord."

Mishael asks, "Who is like God?"

Azariah means "whom the Lord helps."

The Babylonians changed their names in order to transform their identities. With these new names they sought to erase the men's pasts, to abort their destinies, and to convince them to accept their captivity. Daniel's Babylonian name, *Belteshazzar,* means "Baal's prince."

Hananiah was changed to *Shadrach,* which means "under the command of Aku, the moon god."

Mishael was changed to *Meshach,* which asks not, "Who is like God?" but, "Who is like Aku?"

And *Azariah* was changed to *Abednego,* which means "the servant of Nego," another of the Babylon deities.

But putting a new name on the back of their jerseys didn't accomplish squat. Nebuchadnezzar couldn't touch their hearts. They knew who they were. The simple truth is, as long as *you* know who you really are, it doesn't matter what "Babylonian" society calls you, or how much they ridicule you, or what label they place on you. In the immortal words of that famous philosopher, Stanley Burrell (aka. Hammer),

"Can't touch this…"

Bible Teacher and Author Neil Anderson, puts it this way: "Understanding your identity in Christ is absolutely essential to your success at living the victorious Christian life."

Do you want to live in such a way that your life helps transform a generation? Then you have to start by understanding that you are in Christ. It's that simple.

Reforming Your Heart

What does your name mean? Would you change it if you could? If so to what and why?

Do you think your parents had a plan or vision for you when they named you? If so, what does that mean to you; how does it make you feel?

Read Revelation 3: 7-13.

Someone has suggested that all believers have the same last name: Christian. What does this mean to you? Does your lifestyle honor the name of Christ?

Reforming Your Mind

Reflect: *Be honest...what do you think God sees when He looks at you?*

Relate: *I know that the Bible says I am complete in Christ, but I have a really hard time believing that because...*

Reforming Your Actions

Look up the following passages of scripture and make a list of what God says about you.

John 1:12; John 15:15; Romans 5:1; 1 Corinthians 6:17; 1 Corinthians 6:19-20; 1 Corinthians 12:27; Ephesians 1:3-8; Colossians 1:13-14; Colossians 2:9-10; Hebrews 4:14-16.

ðay 8

Grace: It's Not Just a Name for a Girl

So you've made up your mind…you want to learn the language of Babylon. Great! Just keep two things in mind.

First, pay attention to *how you respond* when you find yourself in cultural captivity. For example, everyone knows that school is not an option. Most students believe that school is just a step or two above an Arizonian prison tent camp (mainly because of the food), so that environment qualifies as cultural captivity. Need more proof? Consider this:

- Do you have a choice of the core classes you must take? No.
- Do you have a choice of what times you will attend? No.
- Do you have a choice of what you will be taught? No.

It's all out of your control. But those things aren't nearly as bad as the Babylonian ideas and philosophies that the Department of "Edumacashin" will shove down your throat! Welcome to life behind enemy lines! Not much you or I can do about it. What matters is how you respond to these facts. Will you choose to get up each day and respond as Daniel did—with faith, integrity, commitment, honor, and gentleness? In this, you *do* have a choice! Make it wisely.

The second thing to keep in mind has to do with cultural relevance—*how you relate to* and interact in cultures that are unreceptive or even hostile to your faith. In other words, you can be a jerk or you can be the one person on your campus that everyone knows is a person of integrity and faithfulness, i.e., someone others can count on to be there when needed.

Honestly, Christians in many places around the world are finding themselves cultural captives in spiritual Babylon. But what about the *purpose* behind captivity? What is God doing?

In his book *How Now Shall We Live?* former presidential aide Chuck Colson talks about two different types of grace: saving grace and common grace. Saving grace is the reason you and I can go by the name Christian. It's God reaching out to us, loving us, forgiving us, and calling us His children. Common grace is the reason this sin-infested world is not already a pile of ashes. Common grace prevents sin from devouring us like a Sumo wrestler at an all-you-can-eat buffet. As agents of God's common grace, we are called to help take care of His creation, to uphold the family, to pursue excellence in all things, and to heal and help those suffering from the weight of sin. It is only by God's grace that we are able to accomplish any of these things. Without God's common grace (working through you and me), this world would not last very long. We are, by God's grace, the glue that's holding this heap together. That's a big responsibility. Could this be the answer to our question ("What is God doing?") or is there something more?

Reforming Your Heart

Read 2 Corinthians 6:1–10.

Chances are you've experienced God's saving grace or you wouldn't be reading this book. But what about verses 3–10 of Paul's letter in 2 Corinthians 6? That's common grace. That's true "cultural relevance." Can you say, as Paul, *"We give no offense in anything, that our ministry may not be blamed."*? Does God's grace flow through you in such a way that you are known for being pure, understanding, patient, kind, sincere, loving, and truthful?

Reforming Your Mind

Reflect: *How are you making the world a better place to live?*

Relate: *It really gets on my nerves when people* _____,
but I am going to work on my attitude and learn to be more
_____ *when that happens.*

Reforming Your Actions

Is there a difficult person or situation that you often have to deal
with? Do you typically respond with grace or something else (like
anger, sarcasm, etc.)? Decide today that you will respond with
grace when the situation arises again. Rehearse what you will do
and stick to it.

ðay 9

Whose Fault Is This Mess?

Ever noticed how most Christians tend to be extremist? For example, when a great enemy threatens the people of God (like the terrorists who destroyed the twin towers and killed thousands on September 11,2001), most people in the church tend to have one of two opposite explanations.

- The prophets of doom: "It is the *judgment* of God brought on us for our sins, so we must confess before Him."
- The spiritual warmongers: "It is the *devil* coming in like a flood against the Kingdom and covenant people of God. Consequently we must rise up and take the land!"

The group screaming the loudest is usually the prophets of doom. These are the Christians who have given up all hope, personally and theologically, that things will ever improve. They're a lot like the prophet Jonah; even after the wrath of God has been "appeased," they continue to prophesy doom and destruction. I suppose it has something to do with the fact that these people often have their own "issues" that they haven't ever worked through. Since they have never learned to receive mercy for their own sins, they have a hard time showing mercy for the sins of others.

Of course, it usually doesn't do a lot of good to try to correct these people. A dedicated prophet of doom usually does not receive correction very well. It usually just ticks them off even more and gives them one more reason to whine and say that they are being persecuted by the rest of the church.

On the other end of the spectrum are those believers who are as blindly optimistic as the doomsayers are pessimistic. Without taking the time to really look seriously at the situation, they spout off a bunch of positive confession mumbo-jumbo that would make even the most uncommitted New Ager proud. So they ignore the facts, confess that the problem doesn't really exist (after all, anything less would be a lack of faith), and engage in "spiritual warfare" without ever taking the time to learn what brought about their captivity in the first place.

Although it is very true that the Lord judges His people and that Satan attacks God's people, sometimes neither of these positions may be entirely true. There were times in the history of Israel when an approaching enemy had nothing to do with the Lord's judgment or the devil's attack. It was simply an opportunity for God's people to trust Him to show Himself strong on their behalf as in the story of Jehoshaphat (see 2 Chronicles 20:1–30) and Gideon (see Judges 6–7).

The bottom line is that we must be willing to honestly and sincerely seek the Lord, ask for His wisdom in understanding why we are going through this trial, and then respond according to His promptings. Anything else is sin at worst, foolishness at best.

Reforming Your Heart

Read the story of Jehoshaphat in 2 Chronicles 20:1–30. Instead of fighting, God's people were called to stand still and witness God's salvation. Can you think of a recent example in your own life when God asked you to "stand still" and watch Him work? Was this easy or difficult for you? How does it make you feel to know that a situation is completely out of your control?

Reforming Your Mind

Reflect: *When something goes wrong, are you more likely to believe that it is God's judgment or the devil's attack?*

Relate: *I have to be honest, I usually think that things are going wrong because...*

Reforming Your Actions

Often when things go wrong, we tend to think that God is punishing us for being such lousy Christians. In those times, we need to remember how much God loves us. Why not take a few minutes right now and ask the Lord to wrap His arms around you and remind you of just how "wide and long and high and deep is the love of Christ" toward you (Ephesians 3:18).

ðay 10

Life Lessons from UB

There are at least four key life-lessons that we can learn from Daniel.

Lesson 1: Our Attitude Determines Our Altitude.

You've seen the type before—over-confident, arrogant, foolish. You know, the ones who think they are "All that."

Attitude.

A bad attitude will cause you a lot of grief if you don't correct it. Don't believe it? Read Romans 1:24–28. God got sick of these people's bad attitude and simply removed the restraints that kept them from destroying themselves.

The thing is, God did not have to make any special effort to send judgment on them. Without His restraining grace, they actually brought judgment on themselves by the desires and lust of their own hearts.

Captivity is a humbling experience. Regardless of whether we humble ourselves or are humbled by the finger of God, a changed attitude makes us candidates for a greater outpouring of His grace.

Lesson 2: All Captivity Is Not Created Equal.

When God's people were slaves in Egypt, it was a brutal experience under the hand of Pharaoh. The suffering in Babylonia, by contrast, was relatively light.

You see, the only restraint that Babylon placed on Israel was simple: "Keep quiet about our sins and we'll let you live, play in our yard, and enjoy some of our pleasures." It was a deal Israel couldn't pass up.

So, what was it like being a slave in the greatest civilized city in the world? Well, there was unbridled perversion, rampant promiscuity, and a complete lack of moral restraint. Other than that, it was great! Almost sounds like home, huh?

Of course, a negotiated settlement is just another way of describing a modified surrender. It is the most dangerous form of captivity. It seduces you into believing that you are free when, in fact, you are a captive.

Lesson 3: Captivity Can Become the Catalyst for Change.

"Pastor, I just can't accept it. Why did God let this happen? It isn't fair."

One of the most difficult lessons in life is learning to deal with change—especially when it involves personal loss. Faced with painful change, we often shut down. The result: We stop growing, emotionally and spiritually.

Unfortunately, many present-day Christians never consider that God might be responsible for anything negative that happens in their lives. Yes, we are more than conquerors (Romans 8:37). But to be a conqueror, you have to conquer something. And the truth is that negative situations in our lives would not be so devastating if we began to view every form of change as the opportunity to move forward.

Lesson 4: Captivity Equals Danger and Opportunity.

The word for *crisis* in Chinese is made up of two symbols. The top character represents potential danger; the lower conveys hidden opportunity. Together they convey the idea that every crisis presents the potential for peril and providence. The results of a crisis depend on how we respond to it.

The Hebrew word for crisis, *mashber,* is also used to describe a birth stool, the seat on which a Jewish woman sat as she gave birth. Your crisis can become the birthing ground for unrealized destiny.

What are you doing with the limitations of life? Do you use them to get better, or are you allowing the devastation of captivity to make you bitter? That is why God uses captivity as a means of testing. It sorts out the truly faithful from those who just want to be more comfortable. Those who are faithful in the little things, whether or not these appear to be opportunities, have stumbled onto the keys to their freedom.

Reforming Your Heart

Read James 1:1–12.

Think about your most recent pity-party (come on...we all have them). Looking back, is it easy to see how God used your circumstances to bring about something good in or for you?

Now think about other times when you experienced similar "hard times." Notice any patterns? Could it be that God has something very specific that He wants to teach you...something that you are "bravely" (i.e., stubbornly) refusing to learn?

Reforming Your Mind

Reflect: *What is the main lesson that you feel like God is trying to teach you—one that you are still struggling to learn?*

Relate: *I must admit, when __(inscrt your own regularly scheduled crisis here)__ happens, I have a hard time finding anything good in it. Will you help me by holding me accountable?*

Reforming Your Actions

Sit down at your computer and make yourself a business card. This card should be a constant reminder to you of the "business" that God is trying to do in your life—the one lesson that you seem to have the hardest time learning. Laminate it and keep it with you at all times.

ðay 11

The Culture Connection

Sitting in a hot, dusty classroom, Daniel swallowed the bitter taste in his mouth. He was a prisoner, and he knew it. But for the first time since his capture, he stopped to consider what was *really* going on. Most of his friends had been imprisoned and were doing hard labor. But things were different for Daniel. He had been handpicked to be trained in the University of Babylon. After his training, he would be forced to serve the barbarians who had murdered his people.

It would probably help if you understood a little about the University of Babylon (UB to us). Think Harvard in ancient Babylon. UB was the most influential school in the ancient world. Everybody who was *anybody* attended UB.

But UB wasn't just a posh academic environment. Like America's Ivy League schools, UB was also a religious institution at its core. Almost all Babylonian priests were trained there. These men, upon graduation, became known as the world's leading experts in astrology, divination, magic arts, and prophetic predictions. Think Harry Potter is complete fiction? Think again. UB makes Hogwarts look like a spiritual playground. And the results are nothing as innocent as JK Rawlings would have you believe.

But Daniel was tough. He made up his mind that he would have no part in this indoctrination.

You can sum it up like this (this is worth memorizing, so grab your highlighter):

He refused to be "cultured" by the culture!

Memorized it yet? Good. Now let's talk about what that means for you and me.

To most people the concept of culture is vague. If you look it up, you'll find that culture can mean several things:

- To a biologist *culture* refers to bacteria growing in a petri dish.
- A corporate executive defines *culture* as "the way we do things around here."
- To others, *culture* is being "highbrow"—classical music, art, poetry—all the "finer" things in life.

But the definition that we are looking for goes something like this: The core values of a group of people that affect everything that group says and does (politics, education, economics, art, media, entertainment, athletics, science, etc.).

Now here's the kicker, and since we're almost out of time for today, you've gotta get this pretty quickly: *All cultures are "religious."*

That's extremely important to understand. Even atheistic UB societies have religious core values, in the sense that they believe in and exalt (read that *worship*) a godless worldview.

Take the United States, for example. People come to America not because we are free (although that is a nice fringe benefit). People come to America because we worship at the altar of independence, success, and materialism. Yes, you can find all this and more at the Church of the American Dream.

The question is, *Will you allow this culture to "culture" you*, or will you stand firm for biblical values?

Reforming Your Heart

Read Romans 8.

God loves us and longs to help us. We can make a difference in our culture! But one of the keys to getting God's help is to simply receive it. That means we have to resist the resources of the enemy and submit to the resources of God.

Think about your own UB experience (aka. public school). From day one you've been groomed to serve as a deacon in the Church of the American Dream. What kinds of things is this world offering you that you should be rejecting?

Reforming Your Mind

Reflect: *What are your dreams in life? Have you ever brought those dreams before God and asked Him to examine them to make sure that they are in line with His plan and not the world's?*

Relate: *I've always dreamed of _____. However, after reading today's devo, I realize that my dreams may have been influenced more by culture than God. I want to correct that.*

Reforming Your Actions

Write out your dreams on a piece of paper or a note card. Now begin looking for examples in the Bible of people who have used their dreams to glorify God.

ðay 12

Christ in Culture

Ever had one of those experiences when something you had heard all your life finally makes sense? It's sort of like having your grandma quote some witty little proverb that always seems dumb until the day you finally get it. All of a sudden Grandma is looking pretty smart. Well, books are like that, too.

More than fifty years ago, a German theologian named H. Richard Niebuhr published a book called *Christ in Culture*. Fifty years ago the book barely made a blip on the publishing radar screen. But today it's considered a classic. Although the book isn't the easiest reading in the world, the message is just what we need in the new millenium. Niebuhr says there are five different ways in which Christians can choose to relate to culture.

1. Warfare: Christ Against Culture

This has been the view of most church folk throughout the past hundred years or so. Christians are required to reject anything that is born or expressed in contemporary culture. This backward view is the reason that Christians quit doing anything even remotely artistic—and the reason it has taken us almost a generation to catch up with the rest of the world in terms of creativity and excellence. Some would argue that we still haven't caught up in many areas.

2. Compromise: Christ of Culture

Believe it or not, there are some who believe that the Church and culture are fully compatible. They believe that Christians are to be indistinguishable from the culture. "Besides," they say, "it isn't the world that needs to be changed, but rather Christianity itself. Christianity is too narrow." If the Word of God is right, then this kind of thinking makes God sick to His stomach (see Rev. 3:16).

3. Power: Christ Above Culture

Taken to the extreme, this philosophy allows Christians to equate the Church proper with Christ and set up a church-run government. Think: Roman Empire and, later on, the supremacy of the Catholic Church. Essentially this is the philosophy that is responsible for the creation of one of the most well known articles in America's constitution, the separation of church and state. Muslims and Hindus still allow their churches to take the place of the government...and it ain't a pretty sight.

4. Paradox: Christ and Culture

This was the predominant view of the '80s and '90s and is still the view of many adults. In this view, Christians are said to live in two different worlds (sort of like parallel universes, for you sci-fi fans). One minute you are living in the Christian world and the next you are in the "real" world. Your faith doesn't affect your lifestyle, and your lifestyle doesn't affect your faith. This worldview is the reason former president Bill Clinton could say he was a Christian and still live like he did.

5. Conversion: Christ Transforming Culture

This is the best model of the five. Here, Christ saves and converts people within their own culture, then moves them toward the process of bringing all of culture under His lordship. This really is the present, prophetic mission of the Church. We are called to penetrate the culture, bringing revival, restoration, and reformation. And in order to truly make a difference, we must accept this awesome responsibility.

So how about it? You up for letting Christ use you to transform culture from the inside out?

Reforming Your Heart

Read Matthew 5:13–16.

Someone once said that you may be the only Jesus that some people will ever see and the only Bible that some will ever read. That's a pretty big responsibility, huh? Essentially, that means that you are the only manifestation of Christ in your culture. Are you a good representation of Christ to your family and friends?

Reforming Your Mind

Reflect: *If you were to walk up on a group of friends who were engaged in, shall we say, "less than wholesome" talk, would anyone feel uncomfortable at your presence? Or would they expect you to jump right in?*

Relate: *There is at least one situation where it is really hard for me to let my light shine and it is when...*

Reforming Your Actions

Think about the confession that you just made about letting your light shine. Find someone you trust and respect. Have that person hold you accountable for this situation and to help you learn to shine your light.

ð̵ay 13

Engaging the Culture

I realize this is no surprise to you, but most adults would be shocked to know that the number one problem plaguing the Church today is not sin but irrelevance! As Christians, we are failing to show in practical ways how Jesus Christ is relevant to life at the beginning of the twenty-first century.

So what does it even mean to be a relevant Christian in the midst of cultural quicksand? Well, to answer that we need to do a little word study.

The Latin root of the word *relevant, relevare,* simply means, "to bear upon." Based on that definition, relevant Christians are those who leave a godly mark on the world around them. This means, in part, communicating truth in such a way that it has personal and practical meaning for those who are listening.

Several years ago there was a pastors' conference deep in the jungle of South America. The conference was held in a remote location on the Amazon River. Most of the village pastors traveled by dugout canoe for as much as three days to reach the conference. Many of those precious pastors owned very few possessions apart from their battered old Bibles. Some didn't even own a pair of shoes.

One of the conference speakers was a local Peruvian who attended Bible college in the United States and had recently returned to minister to his people. His message to those village pastors was on the subject of time management.

"You must buy a Daytimer Organizer®," he advised, "and consult it carefully every morning before going to your office."

Daytimers…? Most of these village pastors had never even stepped foot in an office! Some of their villages only had a handful of people living in grass huts. I still have a difficult time believing how out of touch he had become with his *own* culture! He should have known better.

But you know, the sad thing is that many of us have allowed ourselves to become equally out of touch with our culture. Sometimes, being a Christian seems to blind us to what's going on around us. But it doesn't have to be that way. To be relevant—to make a mark on those around us—really only requires two simple priorities. First, *we've got to cut the religious small-talk.* This means we have to open up and talk about the things that are really important to the culture. We have to tackle issues head-on with the truth of God's word. Second, *we must provide practical solutions to the problems others are facing.*

Things are changing, and they are changing faster all the time. There is very little chance that this world will be recognizable ten years from now, even for those born under the sign of the internet. That is why this issue alone—effectively communicating in the language of your culture—will be the greatest of all challenges for the Church in this new millennium.

Reforming Your Heart

Read Acts 17:16–34.

Paul is an excellent example of what it means to understand and relate to others while maintaining a strong commitment to the truth of God's Word.

Do you know your friends well enough—their likes, dislikes, dreams, and frustrations—to be able to share the Gospel with them in a way that they will understand and accept?

Reforming Your Mind

Reflect: *Have you ever used a mutual interest (such as a sport or a certain musical style) to share Christ with someone? How can you improve at sharing your faith by using these tools?*

Relate: *My best experience of really connecting with someone and sharing Christ is...*

Reforming Your Actions

Think of three people you know who aren't Christians. Determine to get to know them well enough to discover a way to introduce them to the good news of salvation in Christ.

ðay 14

I Signed Up to Win, Not Lose

How about some good news? Listen to this...
While many Christians are pessimistic about their ability to influence the direction of American culture, those who oppose Christianity see things a little differently. They regularly rant and rave and raise their blood pressure to meteoric levels while whining about the influence of Christians on popular culture. Among our accomplishments they resent the following examples...

- Hundreds of thousands of churches, Christian schools, and universities, Christian radio and TV stations
- Billions of dollars in contributions to thousands of Christian nonprofit organizations
- Individual Christians infiltrating every aspect of "Babylonian" society

Horrifying stuff, huh? Sends cold chills down your spine just to think about it. :)

Too bad Christians aren't as optimistic about our own potential.

Now let's put this into perspective. Here are three basic principles that should encourage you. Let's call these principles "Kingdom Power Points."

Power Point 1: The power of God is contained within the Gospel.

The apostle Paul said it best:

"For the message of the cross is foolishness to those who are perishing, but to us who are being saved it is the power of God" (1 Corinthians 1:18, nkjv).

When you tell someone about Jesus Christ, it is not just the power of your argument, but also the influence of the Holy Spirit working in and through the message, that can change that person's life.

Stick to the whole truth and nothing but the truth; if you do so, God will help you!

Power Point 2: We do not need to reinvent the message of the Gospel.

Question: If your primary goal is to make it painless for your friends to come to Christ, just where do you draw the line between the negotiables and the nonnegotiables?

Fact is, it still costs to carry the cross. So don't leave out all the hard points like sin, repentance, obedience, and holiness. Dealing with these issues is what characterizes a true disciple.

After all, the rule and reign of Jesus is the only reality that can ever answer the heart cry of man to be loved, valued and nurtured. God's Kingdom is the only truth that gives purpose and meaning to life.

God has already made sure that the Gospel is relevant. You and I simply have to learn how to communicate it to a lost and hurting world so that they hear and understand. So stop fooling with the message…it already works just fine.

Power Point 3: The light of the Gospel is magnified in the darkest place.

Jesus compared our influence on the world to a lit lamp. "Don't put it under a bushel basket," He warned (to paraphrase Matthew 5:15). People who have been isolated in a dark room for a long time squint and shade their eyes at the brightness of even a very small light. As the world we live in becomes darker, more chaotic, and more devoid of character and values, it becomes easier for us to be a dynamic light and witness for Christ. You don't have to perform extraordinary spiritual feats. Just being a normal Christian is radical in the eyes of those around you.

Reforming Your Heart

Read Revelation 22:12–21.

There are many today who think that it is OK to sort of create their own religion. They quote many parts of the Bible, but they leave out all the parts they disagree with. But the Bible is not open for discussion. It is all truth in one package, and if you reject any single part of it, you are rejecting the whole thing.

So, how about it? Any parts of the Bible that you have refused to accept? Now's the time to repent and submit. You'll be better off in the long run.

Reforming Your Mind

Reflect: *Are there any passages or principals in scripture that you have a hard time agreeing with? Why? What are you going to do about this problem?*

Relate: *I wish that __(name a passage or principle)__ weren't true, but I know that it is because it is plainly written in God's Word. So, this is how I'll deal with it...*

Reforming Your Actions

Pray this prayer, keeping God's "hard truths" in mind as you pray: *"Search me, O God, and know my heart; test me and know my anxious thoughts. See if there is any offensive way in me, and lead me in the way everlasting" (Psalm 139:23–24, NIV).*

ðay 15

Jesus, Lord of Culture

Have you ever tried to imagine what the world would be like had man simply obeyed God and stayed away from that stinking fruit tree? I have…and my mind goes blank. I can't even dream up a world where the reality, sovereignty, and glory of God are expressed in all things. But despite my inability to wrap my brain around this concept, it is what God had in mind for Adam, Eve, and all their children—you included. Of course, when man fell this mandate was lost. And it is only in Jesus Christ that the dream can be restored. *When He returns, He will bring to completion the will of God on the earth.* It is in our best interest to get with the program now, while there is still time.

So here's the million-dollar question. Will we wile away our days in frustration or open our eyes to the opportunities God is offering us? This is the greatest time of opportunity and advancement in the history of man. But too many of us seem to be waiting around for the enemy to retreat before we begin laying hands on the sick, casting out demons, clothing the poor, and doing the works of Jesus.

In other words, we're hanging out at the church, waiting for the world to come to us. Besides, it's much safer there, right? The "Babylonian" social challenges of the day seem too great.

But remember this: *We will never change a generation until we are willing to risk it all.*

God is issuing a mandate for His people to disciple the nations with the Word of God. He is looking for radical followers who will arise and step beyond the limitations of previous, powerless generations. He is looking for Daniels who will get involved and make a difference, who will take back everything stolen by the work of the enemy. The time has come to reclaim the arts and sciences, politics and economics, education and athletics, industry, and commerce. As long as we are comfortable with the way things are (i.e., living as cultural captives), we will never change a generation or touch the world for Christ.

So, how do we get started? Well, at the very least, it's gonna take some pioneers who are not just telling others what they ought to do, but who step out in front to cut a path through rugged terrain. You've heard it before—little happens without real leadership. This means pastors, but it also means students, parents, and anyone else with a willing heart and a sense of adventure.

One final thought: Ever noticed that the real leadership in Babylon came from those serving in secular jobs, not religious jobs? Had it not been for a few young Jews in Babylon determined to seize the opportunity of their captivity, Judah would have faded into oblivion, just as Israel had 300 years earlier. That was not the plan of God the Father. He uses people of character willing to be His instruments. Daniel and his friends realized that in order to honor God in a pagan culture, they had to position themselves for dominion.

Captivity is often the catalyst for change. It offers us the opportunity to awaken, replenish our strength, and arise with renewed purpose.

Reforming Your Heart

Read Matthew 10:16–42.

Have you ever had to "step out on a limb" because of your faith? So many Christians around the world are being persecuted every day. Many are being murdered. Chances are, those same scenarios will one day be commonplace in America unless people like you and I work now to prevent it. America's future is not yet written. God doesn't single out Americans in any prophecy. You can change the future by boldly proclaiming Christ today! Together we can make America a country where God is magnified and righteousness rules the day.

Reforming Your Mind

Reflect: *If you could do anything to impact this world for Christ—without restrictions or limitations—what would it be?*

Relate: *I would like to be known as someone who made an impact on this world by...*

Reforming Your Actions

Think about one thing, maybe a hobby, that you love to do and that you think would make a great career (regardless of money). Begin looking for examples of Christians, locally or nationally, who are making a difference for Christ in that career field.

ðay 16

Do You See What I See?

"**I**mpossible!" shouted the king's distinguished panel of astrologers, magicians, and other flakes. How could those four "brats from Judah," who had been eating salads and drinking rainwater, look healthier and stud-lier than those who stuffed their faces at the king's buffet? To make matters worse, the scores from their SATs were in: these guys were ten times smarter than the current leaders in Nebuchadnezzar's kingdom. What was the secret to their wisdom and understanding?

Daniel and his friends struggled to keep straight faces while the king's goons made up excuses. Of course Daniel and his friends had a little secret. Since they were kids, the scribes and elders had taught them the law, and the prophets had stretched their minds to new levels of understanding. In other words, their wisdom was not their own. It was the wisdom of another world. It was the perspective of heaven.

So…what's your perspective? If you had been chosen to walk a mile in Daniel's shoes, would you have fared so well?

Let me help you answer that question, 'cuz it's a thorny one.

Seeing Beyond the Obvious

Every individual has a worldview.

Catch your breath. It's not as "intellectual" as it may sound. Simply put, a worldview is like a pair of glasses. These "shades" give definition and meaning to all you look at—allowing you to interpret the world around you. In other words, your worldview is your basic ideas about how and why things are the way they are. And ideas have consequences.

The goofy looking glasses that your grandparents wore (and probably your parents) made science, reason, and knowledge the most important things. Some people call that "modernism." The consequence of those *modern* ideas was that humans were viewed as nothing more than physical creatures without spiritual, moral, or eternal dimensions. For the modernist, nothing exists beyond the realm of the five senses.

But times they are a-changin'. *Postmodernism* has become the dominant set of eyewear in the Western world.

The postmodernist worldview is very different from the modern worldview. The postmodernist wears flexible lenses that can be bent, stretched, and shaped to fit any lifestyle. Nothing is static. Truth is relative to your situation and subject to whatever feels good for the moment. That's why it's so easy for some folks to say that they are Christian Buddhists or godly homosexuals. It doesn't matter to them that the two things are opposite.

A biblical worldview, by contrast, is based on the eternal Word of God. In the biblical worldview, both science and feelings are subject to the absolute truth as it is revealed in God's word. That was the worldview of Daniel, and it was the key to Daniel's mind-blowing success in front of his Babylonian captors.

So, here's the question again: What's your perspective, or *worldview*? If you had been chosen to walk a mile in Daniel's shoes, would you have fared so well? If you have a solid biblical worldview, the answer is *Yes*.

Reforming Your Heart

"Blessed is the man who does not walk in the counsel of the wicked or stand in the way of sinners or sit in the seat of mockers. But his delight is in the law of the LORD, and on his law he meditates day and night. He is like a tree planted by streams of water, which yields its fruit in season and whose leaf does not wither. Whatever he does prospers" (Psalm 1:1–3, NIV).

The decisions you make, the opinions you carry, the dreams you have: Can they be traced back to a biblical foundation? Is your life really built on the Word of God? If not, you're just asking for trouble. But the flip side is found in Psalm 1—a person who bases her life on God's Word will prosper!

Reforming Your Mind

Reflect: What are the three things in life that are the most important to you? Why? What influence has the Bible had on the way you view those three things?

Relate: *I love the Lord, but I know that some of my decisions about (fill in the blank) have not been based on God's Word. Will you help me correct this?*

Reforming Your Actions

What area of your life has been the least influenced by God's Word? Begin a personal Bible study, researching what the Bible has to say about that issue.

ðay 17

Looking for Truth in All the Wrong Places

Amos 8:11 says that the day will come when God *"will send a famine on the land. Not a famine of bread, nor a thirst for water, but of hearing the words of the LORD.*

God is essentially saying, "Go ahead, smart guy. Do it your way. When you finally get to the place where you feel as though you are starving to hear a word from heaven—when you are desperate enough to hear and obey—then I will open your ears to truth and righteousness."

That's one of those things that should make you go, *Hmmm.*

Go ahead. Try it. *Hmmm.*

Does It Ring a Bell?

Got any friends or relatives you haven't seen in a long time, say five years or more? Strange, isn't it, how people can sometimes change so much that you don't even recognize them.

Or what about the once "favorite toy" that your mom had tucked away in some box in the attic...that you don't even remember.

Funny how time seems to distort and even erase our memories.

So how long has it been since you had an encounter with God's truth? Would you know it if you heard it? Are you even hungry, yet?

You see, our generation has fallen into the trap described by one television commercial that encourages the consumer to "question everything," especially the existence of eternal truth. In following that trend, many Christians do not realize there is a difference between searching for truth and pointing their fingers at God, demanding that He reveal Himself simply to satisfy their cynical curiosity.

Searching for truth is the positive, proactive experience of seeking to know the heart and mind of God, using the Bible as guidebook. *Questioning everything* is the critical attitude of demanding that God produce the evidence we want in order to satisfy our cynicism. Searching for truth is an act of faith. Questioning everything is an act of unbelief. Searching for truth is the act of a sensitive heart that wants to please God. Questioning everything is the act of a hardened heart that wants God to please us. When we search for truth, we meet God on His terms. When we question everything, we demand that God meet us on our terms. Searching for truth brings clarity, wisdom, and insight. Questioning everything just brings more questions until truth eventually becomes unrecognizable.

The Truth Will Set You Free

Perhaps you are wondering, *Isn't this discussion better left to the classrooms of our universities? What does this have to do with my life?* The answer is simple. Your hunger for truth will determine your ability to recognize it when it comes. Remember Amos: God isn't going to speak to you until you are really hungry to listen...and obey! When you start feasting on God's truth, the demons in hell get really nervous. This is why the enemy blinds us to an understanding of the divine design for our lives. To leave us ignorant of God's truth is to leave us captive in spiritual Babylon.

Reforming Your Heart

"Be careful to follow every command I am giving you today, so that you may live and increase and may enter and possess the land that the LORD promised on oath to your forefathers. Remember how the LORD your God led you all the way in the desert these forty years, to humble you and to test you in order to know what was in your heart, whether or not you would keep his commands. He humbled you, causing you to hunger and then feeding you with manna, which neither you nor your fathers had known, to teach you that man does not live on bread alone but on every word that comes from the mouth of the LORD" (Deuteronomy 8:1-3, NIV).

Is reading God's Word a chore for you, or do you honestly enjoy the process? Why do you think this is so?

Reforming Your Mind

Reflect: *Have you ever heard God speak to you...maybe not in an audible way, but you were sure it was Him? What were you doing at the time?*

Relate: *I (have/have not) heard God speak to me through His Word before. Here's why I think this is true...*

Reforming Your Actions

Let's go one step beyond the prayer of Jabez. If you want real power and blessings in your life, pray the prayer of Samuel each day: *"Speak, LORD, for your servant is listening" (1 Samuel 3:9–10).*

ðay 18

Free Your Mind

One of the blockbuster motion pictures of 1999 combined the far-out thinking of sci-fi with the far-out choreography of martial arts action. Next, they threw in a little "despair of mankind" scenario, some cutting edge cinematography and an aggressive soundtrack. The result, though a little tricky at times, was *The Matrix*. Maybe you've heard of it…?

The Matrix was a mind-blowing movie. It took a while before you could even begin to grasp what was going on. In the movie, a race of machines, spawned by artificial intelligence, overtakes the planet and begins the process of systematically eliminating those opposed to its diabolical agenda. In an effort to halt the wholesale slaughter of man, the remaining survivors destroy the atmosphere and darken the sky, believing that these solar-powered machines will be rendered useless. Instead the machines find a new source of energy in human body heat, which they begin to harvest in massive power plants. To keep the crop of captive humans from revolting, they are mentally networked into a virtual world called "the matrix," which simulates earth as we currently know it. Eventually someone discovers the truth and manages to free himself before leading a revolt against the status quo. When this revolutionary dies, it is prophesied that he will return, and that his coming will bring an end to the conflict, thereby freeing humanity.

In its opening weekend *The Matrix,* which is based on the search for and discovery of this reincarnated "messiah," earned over fifty million dollars, and at one point had sold more copies on DVD than any other movie in the history of the United States and Great Britain. A year later, at the 72nd Annual Academy Awards, *The Matrix* surprised everybody by beating Star Wars out of four academy awards: Film editing, visual effects, sounds effects editing and sound. Truly, *The Matrix* reached new heights in sight and sound stimulation.

But why was *The Matrix* so popular? What really compelled people to go see this brainteaser of a movie?

Youth pastors around the United States had a heyday with the film's not-so-subtle spiritual overtones. Film critics loved it. Sci-fi fans loved it. Keanu Reeves fans loved it. Martial arts fans even liked it. But despite the obvious reasons, such as those recognized by the Academy, *The Matrix* seemed to strike a chord on a much deeper level. The movie's theme of "free your mind"—a double entendre used throughout the film—inspired a generation to cast off life's restraints and limitations, whether dictated by others or self-imposed.

But is it really possible to cast off all restraints and totally free your mind? No, not really. You see, the mind works like a matrix, one that has been programmed partly by your Creator and partly by your experience. In the end, we are all slaves to *The Matrix* of the mind. Question is, who's controlling your matrix? Who's controlling the way you view this world? That's possibly one of the most important question's you can ask yourself. Because in the final analysis, only one worldview will produce a life of "righteousness and peace and joy in the Holy Spirit" (Romans 14:17), and that is the one controlled by God and His holy Word.

Reforming Your Heart

"For though we live in the world, we do not wage war as the world does. The weapons we fight with are not the weapons of the world. On the contrary, they have divine power to demolish strongholds. We demolish arguments and every pretension that sets itself up against the knowledge of God, and we take captive every thought to make it obedient to Christ" (2 Corinthians 10:3–5, NIV).

If it were possible to take your thoughts, opinions, and ideas and turn them into a single landscape photo, how much of that landscape would resemble the one painted from God's Word? Are you willing to "take captive every thought to make it obedient to Christ?"

Reforming Your Mind

Reflect: *If someone were to point out that your opinion was not in line with God's Word, would you be offended, repentant or indifferent? Why?*

Relate: *I remember a time when my (name person/relationship) challenged my beliefs about _____. It made me feel...*

Reforming Your Actions

Think of a popular opinion among your friends that is not in line with the Word of God. Ask God to show you how you can use the weapons of the Spirit (the Word of God and prayer) to demolish that stronghold.

ðay 19

Can You See it, Man?

OK, so we've established the fact that without a biblical worldview, you're toast. So, what exactly does a biblical worldview look like? Well, there are at least seven main components of a biblical worldview.

1. God Is the One True and Sovereign God.

The belief that God exists is not unique to the Christian faith. A lot of people believe in some sort of divine entity or supernatural force. But only Christians believe in the one true, sovereign, and personal God who loves and cares for His children. When you reject God as your heavenly Father, you destroy your only hope for purpose in this life.

"What we believe about God," said the great revivalist A. W. Tozer, "is the most important thing about us." Our understanding of God, no matter how limited, determines our actions, attitudes, and worldview.

And it is that belief, above all others, that sets Christianity apart.

2. Evil Is Present and Unavoidable in the World.

The greatest enemy of the human race is Satan and the forces of darkness. But many consider belief in the existence of a personal devil as naive, unsophisticated, even primitive.

In spite of our blindness to the work of evil in the world, Satan lives with the agenda of destroying everything God intended for His pleasure. That means that no matter where you go in life, you will face challenges. The romantic notion of living in relationship with Jesus Christ as a way of avoiding the challenges of life is dangerous. The scriptures teach the opposite. To live righteously is to invite the wrath of the kingdom of darkness. It is unavoidable.

3. The Mercy of God Is Freely Offered to Man.

Many people picture God as distant, indifferent to the needs of mortals until we can somehow move Him to action through our desperate cries of pain.

The Bible, by contrast, reveals a sovereign God who, long before we ever sinned, reached out to us. Although we are undeserving, the mercy of God is offered freely to us through the life of Jesus Christ. No more lonely nights. No more going it alone. Thanks to the work of Christ on the cross of Calvary, we can be restored to our intended place with God.

4. Man Is Chosen, Fallen, and Redeemed.

God designed you and me to live in righteousness, but the disobedience of Adam and Eve forever changed mankind. David said, "Indeed, I was born guilty, a sinner when my mother conceived me" (Psalm 51:5, NRSV). Although we were created to rule and reign, we entered life as slaves to sin and unrighteousness.

But the story doesn't end there—thank the Lord! Because of God's love for us, a love so deep that it seems almost impossible to understand, we've been given a second chance. Yes we were born in sin, but God, who is rich in mercy, has made a way for us to be redeemed.

Reforming Your Heart

"As for you, you were dead in your transgressions and sins, in which you used to live when you followed the ways of this world and of the ruler of the kingdom of the air, the spirit who is now at work in those who are disobedient. All of us also lived among them at one time, gratifying the cravings of our sinful nature and following its desires and thoughts. Like the rest, we were by nature objects of wrath. But because of his great love for us, God, who is rich in mercy, made us alive with Christ even when we were dead in transgressions—it is by grace you have been saved" (Ephesians 2:1–5, NIV).

Paul says, in essence, that the devil rules this world and has power over everyone who doesn't obey God. Do you find that easy to believe or hard to believe? Why?

Reforming Your Mind

Reflect: *Do you remember the first time you asked God to forgive you of your sins? How did you feel afterwards?*

Relate: *Let me tell you what the love of God as my heavenly Father means to me...*

Reforming Your Actions

"No more lonely nights. No more going it alone." That's a message your friends and loved ones need to hear. Find someone today with whom you can share the love and mercy of God.

ðay 20

Can You Still See It, Man?

Yesterday we began looking at the seven main components of a Christian worldview. Let's review:

1. **God the Father Is the One True and Sovereign God.**
2. **Evil Is Present and Unavoidable in the World.**
3. **The Mercy of God Is Freely Offered to Man.**
4. **Man Is Chosen, Fallen, and Redeemed.**

Now let's take a look at the last three components.

5. Jesus Christ Is the Only Path to Eternal Life.

Two thousand years ago the birth of Jesus Christ divided time and changed the world forever.

"I am *the* way and *the* truth and *the* life." Jesus said. "No one comes to the Father except through me" (John 14:6, emphasis added).

Notice that He did not claim to *have* the way, or even to *know* the way; He claimed to *be* the way. That one claim is enough to set Him apart from every other religious leader in history.

Of course, that kind of absolute, intolerant thinking clashes with the postmodern mind. In a pluralistic culture, many people choose to identify Jesus as a prophet, or even a good, moral man, while refusing to acknowledge Him as the only begotten Son of God. But that boat won't float. Think about it. If He was not who He claimed to be—the Son of God, coequal with the Father—then that makes Him a liar (or a lunatic). How could a person like that still be considered a good moral teacher?

6. The Holy Spirit Is Actively at Work in the World.

Of the three Persons in the Godhead—Father, Son, and Holy

Spirit—the Spirit is probably the least known and understood. Yet it is the Holy Spirit who acts as the "executive agent" of the Godhead. The Father *wills,* the Son *reveals,* and the Spirit *makes it happen.* He draws us to the Father, baptizes us into Christ, fills us with power, and leads us into spiritual maturity. Not only is He involved with us individually, but also the Spirit is responsible for the development of the Church in this present age and for restraining the flood of evil that would otherwise overwhelm the world.

7. The Kingdom of God Is Destined to Prevail over Every World System.

When Communists assumed control of China in 1947, the regime expelled every foreign missionary from the nation. Many faithful believers were forced to leave, fearing that the demonic forces of Communism would destroy the work of God. To many the battle seemed lost. Yet forty years later, when China was reopened to foreign visitors, a thriving underground church was evident. The powers of Communism were no match for the rule and reign of Jesus Christ.

It's not always easy to recognize God at work in the world, but rest assured, He *is* at work and He *will* prevail. Christianity is the only religion with the real power to change the planet. When God's people embrace a biblical worldview, the impact on the world is unavoidable.

Reforming Your Heart

" 'But what about you?' [Jesus] asked. 'Who do you say I am?' Simon Peter answered, 'You are the Christ, the Son of the living God.' Jesus replied, 'Blessed are you, Simon son of Jonah, for this was not revealed to you by man, but by my Father in heaven. And I tell you that you are Peter, and on this rock I will build my church, and the gates of Hades will not overcome it' " (Matthew 16:15–18, NIV).*

Read that passage again. What is the "rock" that Jesus was talking about? Upon what has Jesus built His church?

(Hint: It is NOT Peter himself, but it has something to do with worldview component five, and it is right here in this passage!)

Reforming Your Mind

Reflect: *Have you received the Holy Spirit since you put your faith in Christ? (See Acts 19:1–6.)*

Relate: *I am still learning to follow the lead of the Holy Spirit. I still struggle with...*

Reforming Your Actions

Jesus is either a liar, or a lunatic, or He truly is the Son of God, coequal with the Father. Commit this fact (and its earlier explanation) to memory today. Be ready to share this foundational truth with someone in need.

ðay 21

Agent 3:16

That Nebuchadnezzar was such a great guy. He gave those piti-ful Jews a nice little ghetto to live in while they helped him build his cities. It was a fabulous arrangement: The Jews were free to live in the security of their own, uh, "communities," while being able to rely completely on the nice Babylonians for food, shelter, and protection. Those greedy Jews should have been thankful. Instead, many abandoned hope.

Of course, most of us would have felt the same way. Being a slave is simply not the career choice of most people.

But Daniel...well, he viewed things a little, let's use the word *differently*. He never once thought of himself as a slave. Instead, he used the system for God's advantage. He started looking for ways to infiltrate the Babylonian society. I guess you could say Daniel was the James Bond of his day. Agent 001.

So if Daniel—whose situation was much worse than any you and I are likely to face in our lifetimes—can learn how to make a difference in his world, what's our problem? I think the main prob-lem is bad theology.

"Oh no...not the *T-word*," he said, with a pained expression on his face.

Relax. This will be relatively painless. Let me boil it down for you: *We have misinterpreted a number of scriptures, like the one that warns us not to be friends with the world (James 4:4).*

Huh?

Keep reading, pilgrim, and you'll see what I mean.

So What Exactly Is "the World"?

The Bible has several different ways in which the word *world* is defined, depending on the passage it is used in. Take a look.

Creation—"[Jesus] was in the world, and the world was made through Him…" (John 1:10).

Humanity—"For God so loved the world" (John 3:16).

Sinners—"I pray for them. I do not pray for the world, but for those You have given Me, for they are Yours" (John 17:9).

Culture—"Adulterers and adulteresses! Do you not know that friendship with the world is enmity with God?" (James 4:4).

So, when understood correctly, it seems obvious. We have to be in the culture, we just can't let the culture be in us. *In*, not *of*.

The Myth of Separation

So we got our theology a little mixed up. So what, right? Wrong. The result is that we've created an artificial wall between the *secular* and the *sacred*. Once you buy into a secular-versus-sacred way of thinking, you begin to compartmentalize your faith. In other words, you start believing that prayer, worship, and ministry must be separated from the "secular" aspects of life such as work, marriage, politics, education, and athletics (to name just a few). But as far as God is concerned, there is no difference between spiritual work and secular work. A. W. Tozer once wrote, "The man who walks with God will see and know that for him there is no strict line separating the sacred from the secular."[1]

The bottom line is that we all have been called to be priests…only the pulpit changes. Whether you want to be a doctor or a salesman, an engineer or a teachers, you have a responsibility to preach the good news to those in your reach.

And that's how you become an agent of change, like Daniel. Agent 3:16…that's you.

Reforming Your Heart

"For we are His workmanship, created in Christ Jesus for good works, which God prepared beforehand that we should walk in them" (Ephesians 2:10).

Think about some of the Christian adults you know who are already well-established in their careers, be they politics or restaurant management. How are these men and women of faith using their positions as a way of introducing people to the good news of Jesus Christ?

Now bring it home. You may have several years before you settle into a career, but you already have the power to influence your world. How are you using your position—classes, hobbies, sports, clubs—to be a witness of God's love?

Reforming Your Mind

Reflect: *What's one thing you could do differently that would allow you to be more effective as an "Agent 3:16" in your world?*

Relate: *I often miss opportunities to share God's love with others because...*

Reforming Your Actions

Go on a "spy" mission today. As you go through your regular routine, look for holes in the devil's defenses that would allow you to begin sharing God's love with the people around you. Make a note of these opportunities and begin asking God for wisdom in approaching each one.

ðay 22

Twister

Daniel had been taught the commandments from childhood. The first and foremost is found in Deuteronomy: "I am the LORD your God who brought you out of the land of Egypt, out of the house of bondage. You shall have no other gods before Me" (Deut. 5:6, NKJV).

Did you catch that? The first commandment to worship the God of Abraham exclusively was introduced with the phrase "out of the land of Egypt." The commandment had not changed in hundreds of years, but the situation had. Now Israel was *back* in captivity, only this time it was Babylon instead of Egypt.

Think about it. In an unimaginable turn of events, Israel's elite had once again become slaves and were being trained this time in the language, art, literature, and civilization of their captors—Babylon. Talk about culture shock! For someone who loved God and was dedicated to His service, it was the ultimate humiliation. If God wanted to teach Daniel how to stand against the winds of a pagan culture, He did so by throwing him into the middle of a Babylonian tornado.

Now here's the real danger. In situations such as this one, it's easy to start making excuses for your behavior. Compromise gets easier and easier with each new day. A slip here, a nudge there, an overlooked action or two, and eventually you find yourself smack in the middle of a values storm. The things you once believed, the values you once held dear, get tossed mercilessly by the winds of what it seems you must do in order to get ahead—or maybe just to survive. When Daniel and his friends refused to eat the king's meat, I am sure many of the other Jews had some strong advice for them.

"What do you guys think you're doing? You're going to get us all killed! This is no time to be self-righteous, and it's not a good idea to complain about the king's food. Can't you see God has spared our lives by bringing us here? Why would He have allowed us to be brought here if He didn't want us to eat the king's meat? Look, everyone else is eating it."

Ouch. That's gotta hurt. Maybe you've been there. Maybe you've been in a situation or two where you felt pressured on all sides, blown around by the winds of the culture and by the "good intentions" of your friends. How do you hang on? How do you keep from being whisked away in this values storm and ending up like some sort of Wizard of Oz play-toy at the mercy of the wicked witch of Babylon?

Well, if Daniel's life is any indication of what to do, then it seems the pathway to dominion, the key to true cultural impact, is to "serve your way into a place of responsible influence." It is knowing when to sit quietly and when to take a stand for principles. And let me warn you: That's impossible without a firm knowledge of God and His Word. Those who have only casually followed Christ will simply be swept away in the storm.

Reforming Your Heart

"If any of you lacks wisdom, he should ask God, who gives gener-ously to all without finding fault, and it will be given to him. But when he asks, he must believe and not doubt, because he who doubts is like a wave of the sea, blown and tossed by the wind. That man should not think he will receive anything from the Lord; he is a double-minded man, unstable in all he does" (James 1:5-8, NIV).

Think about some of the "values wars" that you've been in. Values wars are those times when you find yourself in the middle of a conflict over what you believe is wrong and what those around you are insisting is right (or vice-versa).

Looking back, can you think of some battles where it would have been better to walk away? Can you think of some times when you wish you had taken a stronger stand? What can you learn from those experiences that will help you during the next conflict?

Reforming Your Mind

Reflect: *Have you ever been in a situation where what you believed was being ridiculed or attacked? How did you respond?*

Relate: *I have a really hard time keeping quiet when someone __(tell what and why)__ .*

Reforming Your Actions

Think of someone you know who is antagonistic toward you and your beliefs. Now think of a way to serve that person. Do it!

ðay 23

Receive, Retreat, Reform

Daniel's ability to make a difference in Babylon all came down to one decision based on three options. We, too, must face the same three options:

1. to *receive* the culture as the standard of conduct for our lives
2. to *retreat* from the culture in a callous state of indifference
3. to *reform* the culture by demonstrating the Lordship of Christ in every arena of life.

Option 1: Receiving the Culture

Christians who receive the culture are those who love the world, but not the way God loves it. Remember Lot's wife: She loved Sodom so much that she just *had* to look back. Bad decision.

If we could read into the story of Lot's wife, we would say that she no longer lived what she said she believed. Her feet seemed to follow God but her heart was in Sodom. Maybe you know someone like that. Sure, they go to church every Sunday. They may even go more often than that. But when it comes to decisions that require a strong moral compass, they wind up on the wrong side of the woods, if you know what I mean. They become living examples of what's wrong with many churches today; you can't tell them apart from the sinners they hang out with.

If you do not live what you believe, your words have no power to transform people's lives. That is one of the effects of letting the culture get "in you." You lose your unique identity, and your witness is so watered down with compromise that you lack the power to affect anyone.

Option 2: Retreating from the Culture

Think of a castle set up on a hill, complete with fortifications, moat and drawbridge. It strategically overlooks the city below—the habitat of sinners. People have retreated to the castle to worship God, to fellowship with one another, and to escape the corruption of the world. They have been redeemed, cleansed, and filled. They have a passion for purity, righteousness, and even true worship that is pleasing to God. They want to be all God wants them to be. They want high standards.

The folks up in the castle are good people and would love for all their old friends from the city to join them. They used to send out commando evangelists to rescue their lost friends. But there were too many close calls, too much risk of contamination. So they went back to the old strategy of lobbing Gospel mortar shells from their tactical position in the castle.

It is difficult, if not impossible, to genuinely care for the people of the culture if we are concentrating our efforts on staying away from them. We become like the priest in the story of the Good Samaritan. We avoid the sinners at all cost, becoming "so heavenly minded that we are no earthly good."

Obviously, neither of these choices—retreating or receiving—is acceptable. Tomorrow we'll talk about the third option: learning to *reform* the culture.

Reforming Your Heart

"Do not love the world or anything in the world. If anyone loves the world, the love of the Father is not in him. For everything in the world—the cravings of sinful man, the lust of his eyes and the boasting of what he has and does—comes not from the Father but from the world. The world and its desires pass away, but the man who does the will of God lives forever" (1 John 2:15–17, NIV).

Are there still areas of your life where you have a "love" for this world? How can you be sure?

"For, 'Everyone who calls on the name of the Lord will be saved.' How, then, can they call on the one they have not believed in? And

how can they believe in the one of whom they have not heard? And how can they hear without someone preaching to them?" (Romans 10:13–14, NIV).

Have you seen someone in need lately and "passed by on the other side?" Are you sure?

Reforming Your Mind

Reflect: *As a Christian, what is one thing this world offers that is the greatest temptation to you?*

Relate: *When I see people in this situation ___(describe it)___, I want to help, but I'm afraid or nervous about helping because...*

Reforming Your Actions

Think of something that you can "give up" for the remainder of this spiritual adventure. For example, if you listen to secular music, try listening to Christian music only for the next twenty-six days. Keep a diary of your experience.

ðay 24

The Qualities of a Reformer

Daniel refused to either receive or retreat from the culture that held him captive. Instead, he determined to learn its language so he could be a reformer. Here are seven practical pointers we can learn from Daniel about turning our captivity into an opportunity to infiltrate the culture as a witness for Christ.

1. Daniel Entered the Culture with the Outcome in View.

Daniel resolved not to defile himself (Daniel 1: 8). If you start down this road without being crystal clear about your absolute allegiance, you will gradually be absorbed and transformed into a Babylonian. You must count the cost early on.

2. Daniel Chose His Battles Carefully.

Daniel separated the negotiables from the nonnegotiables.

He allowed them to change his name, because he knew who he really was. He accepted their Babylonian education because he knew what he believed. But when they demanded that he eat the king's meat, he appealed to their better judgment. When they required him to stop praying to Jehovah, he defied their orders. Even in his youth Daniel had the ability to distinguish between a cultural preference and a clear-cut violation of God's command.

Sometimes zealous Christians take bold, uncompromising stands on issues that are relatively insignificant and just wind up looking weird, arrogant, and self-righteous. People who major in minors do so because they are more interested in making a statement than in making a disciple. What good is it if you change all the rules to accommodate your beliefs when, in the end, everyone hates you and what you believe as well?

It takes wisdom, discernment, and divine guidance to figure out when to dig in and take a stand and when to fall back and fight another day. As we said earlier, those who don't really know God's Word and who have followed Christ only casually will have a hard time determining where to draw that line.

3. Daniel Was Not Afraid to Challenge the Status Quo.

You know the story. When the Babylonians brought Daniel his first meal, Daniel asked the chief official for permission "not to defile himself this way" (Daniel 1:8). The commander feared that if Daniel and his friends were not healthy, Nebuchadnezzar would literally have his head. Daniel responded, "Please test your servants for ten days..." (Daniel 1:12–13). It worked, and Daniel and his friends were able to take a stand for what they believed in. As a matter of fact, at the end of three years, the king examined the four young men. "In all matters he found them ten times better" than any of the kings men (Daniel 1:20). Daniel did not use his religious preferences as an excuse for a lack of excellence.

Tomorrow we'll look at four more qualities we can learn from Daniel about turning our captivity into an opportunity to infiltrate the culture as a witness for Christ.

Reforming Your Heart

"Dear friends, I urge you, as aliens and strangers in the world, to abstain from sinful desires, which war against your soul. Live such good lives among the pagans that, though they accuse you of doing wrong, they may see your good deeds and glorify God on the day he visits us" (1 Peter 2:11–12, NIV).

What are they saying about you when your back is turned? Are they accusing you of being godly? Are they blasting you for being righteous, or for being smug? When their eyes are opened to the truth (either now or on judgement day), will they glorify God because of the way you lived your life?

Reforming Your Mind

Reflect: *What are the "nonnegotiables" for you—the areas in which you refuse to compromise?*

Relate: *I know that if I take a stand on this issue __(identify the issue)__ it could cost me...*

Reforming Your Actions

It may be the latest craze, but you know it's not the right thing to be a part of. Whatever that thing may be, make a decision today that you will not follow the crowd on this one.

ðay 25

"Reformers"- the Sequel

Yesterday, we looked at the first three qualities of a reformer based on Daniel's example.

1. **Daniel Entered the Culture with the Outcome in View.**
2. **Daniel Chose His Battles Carefully.**
3. **Daniel Was Not Afraid to Challenge the Status Quo.**

Here are four more practical pointers we can learn from Daniel about turning our captivity into an opportunity to infiltrate the culture as a witness for Christ.

4. Daniel Exemplified Sincere Spirituality.

Daniel was not just religious; he was a truly spiritual man who sought God through every stage of his life.

The king had been tormented by a recurring dream and none of his magicians were able use their tricks to solve the puzzle. Only Daniel was able to reveal the dream in detail and interpret it. Why? Because Daniel's relationship with God was more than talk: He walked the walk.

The world is looking for people with a genuine relationship with God. They are turned off by anything they perceive as pretense. This is about more than simply following some religious rules and regulations. You can follow all the rules but be backsliding in your heart. People who find themselves in this situation have usually developed a lifestyle around the regulations. As with the Pharisees, the "law" of God is no longer a spiritual challenge; it is a habit.

5. Daniel Saw Himself as an Instrument of the Sovereign God.

God puts people in positions of power and influence. It happens at appointed times for a particular purpose. The problem is when these people make it to "the top," they can become territorial, compromising in order to maintain what they have achieved. They are not willing to risk their position or their relationships in order to take a stand for Christ.

Maybe you've seen this before. A Christian friend is elected president of the student body or captain of the cheerleading team. So far so good, right? But the position seems to change your friend. Soon your friend is dressing, talking, and living like the sinners she used to pray for. She forgot that she was placed in her position by God to be an influencer, *not* to be influenced.

But the lives and actions of Daniel and his friends are just the opposite. Sure, they had great successes, but they remained surrendered to God—and it could have cost them everything. Daniel faced the lions' den for his stance. Shadrach, Meshach, and Abednego faced the fiery furnace for theirs. To be an effective infiltrator you have to be willing to put it all on the line when the situation calls for it.

6. Daniel and His Friends Positioned Themselves for Greatness, Even at Personal Risk.

Take a moment to read Daniel 3:28–29. Despite their refusal to become part of the culture, the three Hebrew men were promoted yet again!

And Daniel himself? What became of him when he refused to pray to anyone but Jehovah? Read Daniel 6:26–28. The scripture says he "prospered" (verse 28).

7. Daniel Refused to Play the Humanistic Advancement Game.

God used Daniel and his friends to infiltrate and influence a pagan culture in a way that is unprecedented in history. But neither Daniel nor his friends did any of the things that we tend to do in order to get ahead. They were simply full of character, faithful, and dedicated to what they believed. And they took the Kingdom of God to the highest levels in the land of the enemy.

So what about it, Christian? Do you have the qualities of a reformer? If not, it's never too late to get started down the right path.

Reforming Your Heart

"Faith by itself, if it is not accompanied by action, is dead. But someone will say, 'You have faith; I have deeds.' Show me your faith without deeds, and I will show you my faith by what I do...As the body without the spirit is dead, so faith without deeds is dead" (James 2:17–18, 26 NIV).

Do your actions match your words? Do you walk the walk and talk the talk? When people talk about you, can they rightly accuse you of being a hypocrite?

Reforming Your Mind

Reflect: *Why do you think people change when they get into certain positions or clubs?*

Relate: *I would love to be in __(name a club or group__), but I am not willing to do this __(describe)__ in order to get in.*

Reforming Your Actions

Look around. Is there something in your school or neighborhood that you've always wanted to do, such as be on the student council or act as a team leader? Write out a list of things you would do for Christ if you were in that position.

ðay 26

You've Been Recruited

A good job has always been hard to find.
During the time of Daniel's captivity, the best job around was to be one of the king's many soothsayers. You know, a professional wacko, a palm reader, a tarot card totin', psychic hotline hoggin' wacko. They had the highest pay, the highest benefits, and the lowest required skill levels. In other words, they were all scam artists. I suppose the ancient world wasn't so different from today.

Many cultures in the ancient world practiced occultism, but the Babylonians distinguished themselves by institutionalizing the magic arts as part of their government (see Daniel 2:2). They were particularly known throughout the world for their reliance on astrology. Day in and day out, the magicians, astrologers, and sorcerers lied to the nation and even to the king—and got away with it!

But Daniel's presence had somehow shifted the cosmic order and caused the yin-yang balance of eternal nirvana to move beyond the realm of positive energy flow through the intergalactic astral plane.

Sorry. I couldn't resist.

What I meant to say was that the wackos were striking out. Nebuchadnezzar had changed his tactics and there was no way they could deceive him this time. Suddenly the psychic readers forgot how to read. So ol' Neb had them all executed.

Yep, a good job is hard to find.

That's when Daniel stepped up to the plate. The king needed answers and Danny Boy knew the Source. It was time to start turning things around.

Crossing the Line of Indifference

Fast forward a couple thousand years.

Bankhead Courts Public Housing Project had been forsaken by the city of Atlanta and overtaken by drug dealers, prostitutes, and gang members. The Atlanta Housing Authority had written to a hundred churches asking for help...without a single response.

But when Southern Bell temporarily suspended repair service and the U.S. Postal Service halted mail delivery, Bishop Earl Paulk decided something had to be done. Rising to the pulpit one Sunday morning, he issued a challenge to his 12,000 parishioners to "adopt" Bankhead Courts.

Patty Battle responded to the challenge...and forever changed the community of Bankhead Courts.[1]

Relevant Christians in a Changing World

What does it mean to serve as a relevant Christian in contemporary society? According to Harvard professor Paul Tillich, it means that the Christian message answers the basic questions of humanity today. "Irrelevant" means that it does not answer those questions.[2]

So, what questions are we talking about? Simple. Things such as:

What does it mean to be a human?

Where do I get the courage to live?

How can I have hope? And for what?

How can I overcome the conflicts that torture my heart and mind?

These questions could also be called passionate quests for a meaningful life.[3]

The only way to answer these questions for a lost and hurting world is to draw a line in the sand and step over it...just as Daniel did in Babylon; just as Patty Battle did in Bankhead Courts. The mandate to infiltrate and transform the world in which we live is the responsibility of every individual Christian. Whether you are leading Cub Scouts or a congregation, you need to follow the pattern of Jesus and engage the culture for the purpose of transformation.

Reforming Your Heart

"David asked the men standing near him, "What will be done for the man who kills this Philistine and removes this disgrace from Israel? Who is this uncircumcised Philistine that he should defy the

armies of the living God?...Your servant has killed both the lion and the bear; this uncircumcised Philistine will be like one of them, because he has defied the armies of the living God" (1 Samuel 17:26, 36, NIV).

It takes the courage of a David or a Daniel to step up to the plate and go to bat against the forces of darkness. Do you have what it takes? Would you like to find out?

Reforming Your Mind

Reflect: *Have you ever been tempted to call a psychic hotline or follow your horoscope? Why?*

Relate: *I think people pay money to scam artists like psychics because...*

Reforming Your Actions

On your way to and from school, look around your community. What needs are obviously going unmet? What groups or neighborhoods are being ignored and could use your help?

ðay 27

Possessing the Land

Abraham Kuyper was a man of many talents: a prime minister and statesman, a pastor, theologian, journalist, philosopher, and the founder of the Free University of Amsterdam in 1880. Needless to say, he was a pretty smart guy.

Kuyper was convinced that the sovereignty of God and the Lordship of Jesus Christ governed the affairs of history. Now you may be wondering, *How can anyone with a brain say that God is responsible for the mess this world is in?*

Well just hold on there, little buckaroo, and let's see if we can figure out what this guy meant.

First of all, Kuyper believed that Christ was sent to redeem every aspect of society, and that the Church is left with the responsibility to complete what He initiated.

Kuyper once said, "There is not one square inch in the whole domain of our human existence over which Christ, who is Sovereign over all, does not cry: 'Mine!'"[1] It's this cry, this clarion call, that the Church is expected to answer to. Our goal, then—if Kuyper is right—is to restore some of what was lost since the Israelites crossed over into the promised land. It is a call to possess the land.

This idea formed the basis for Kuyper's teaching, which he called "sphere sovereignty." Kuyper believed that God is sovereign over each of the seven basic areas of life—state government, family, religion, business vocation, education, science, and the arts.

One thing Kuyper did not do was distinguish between the sacred and the secular. Because of his belief that God was sovereign over all, he saw all things as sacred. He saw the world as the stage on which the drama of God's supreme will is displayed.

Let's take a brief look at each of the seven realms of sovereignty. Hopefully, this will awaken you to the driving purpose behind our need to learn the language of Babylon. Remember: It takes both common grace and saving grace to preserve, restore, and reform a culture or nation.

The First Sphere

Kuyper described, first of all, the sphere of state authority or government as an area of life over which God does and must reign supreme.

William Wilberforce, a member of Parliament for forty-five years, was one of Britain's great world changers. Wilberforce was converted to Christ after consciously resisting the love of God for years. Why did he resist? Because he believed, as many do, that if he became a Christian he would have to abandon his political aspirations and give up his circle of friends. He wanted both.

But thanks to the sound advice of John Newton, who was then an Anglican priest and the author of many hymns, including "Amazing Grace," Wilberforce stayed in politics. Eventually he became the most influential figure in the movement resulting in the abolition of slavery in Britain.

Even though the government does not have the answers to society's problems, we desperately need men and women of godly character in this dark hour to serve their nations and make a difference...like John Wilberforce.

Reforming Your Heart

"Yours, O LORD, is the greatness and the power and the glory and the majesty and the splendor, for everything in heaven and earth is yours. Yours, O LORD, is the kingdom; you are exalted as head over all. Wealth and honor come from you; you are the ruler of all things. In your hands are strength and power to exalt and give strength to all" (1 Chronicles 29:11–12, NIV).

Is God really the head over all things? Does He rule your heart? your dreams? your plans? your decisions? your day? your future?

He can't be the God over the affairs of our land (government) until He is the God over the affairs of our hearts.

Reforming Your Mind

Reflect: *When someone talks about the sovereignty of God, how does that make you feel? Why?*

Relate: *If I were on the student council, I would use my position as a way to influence our school for Christ by...*

Reforming Your Actions

Spend time in prayer today for the president and any other political leaders you can think of. Specifically, ask God to place His people in positions of influence in our country.

ðay 28

The Second Sphere

Yesterday we started talking about Abraham Kuyper's ideas on "sphere sovereignty." The first sphere looked at government. The second sphere looks at social circles and is divided into six remaining areas of life: family, religion, business vocation, education, science and the arts. Today let's look at our mission in the family, church, and work.

Our Mission in the Family

Think of the family as the DNA of society. As the family goes, so goes the church and the rest of society. And right now, it's going in the wrong direction.

Alternative lifestyles, sexual immorality, economic concerns and the feminist agenda have wreaked havoc on the family. The enemy has so distorted God's plan for the family and society that even the most conservative-minded people are confused. Many are tempted to modify the blueprint, to make it more "modern." But as ancient as God's plan may seem, every other plan is guaranteed to fail. The so-called alternative lifestyles that we see around us will eventually lead to poverty of soul and to death. We must restore the rule of God in our families.

Our Mission in the Church

Let's face it folks, the Church is in trouble. Reformation is needed from the inside out. All of our attention and energy has become fixed on nonessentials. Instead of figuring out ways to inject the truth of the gospel into the veins of a dying world, we've spent billions of dollars and millions of hours on making ourselves more attractive. Dying people don't need to see your pretty new coat or hear your stories about how hip and non-religious you are. They need *His* blood…and it flows through your spiritual veins.

It's time for the Church to rise up and be the Church again. We must restore the rule of God in our church and quit letting the world tell God how to do His business.

Our Mission in Business and Industry

Catholicism urged people to live in convents and monasteries. But the Reformers, particularly John Calvin, argued that Christians did not need to be separated from the world in order to render Christian service. Bakers, carpenters, farmers, and artisans could all serve God in their respective activities if they were able to view their work as a primary means of serving God. Even the most ordinary of jobs can become "sacred" if the results testify to the faith of the workers. What does your work say about your faith? Do people see the good job that you do and—knowingly or unknowingly—give God the glory?

Like it or not, your job is the broadest platform you will ever have to communicate the grace and faithfulness of God. Think about it:

- Do your co-workers struggle with the purpose and meaning of their lives and careers?
- Are you working with people who are sick, depressed, tormented, confused, hopeless, and away from God?

If the answer to these questions is *yes*, then you have been given a great opportunity to minister! Like a modern-day Daniel, we must restore the rule of God in our jobs and help our bosses solve their toughest problems. Are you available?

Reforming Your Heart

"You are the light of the world. A city built on a hill cannot be hid. No one after lighting a lamp puts it under the bushel basket, but on the lampstand, and it gives light to all in the house. In the same way, let your light shine before others, so that they may see your good works and give glory to your Father in heaven" (Matthew 5:14–16, NRSV).

120

We know that the world seems bent on destroying God's plan for the family, but what about you? Do you show honor and respect to your parents? Do you prioritize your family relationships over your relationships with your friends? Do you accept any responsibility for keeping your family strong?

Reforming Your Mind

Reflect: *What do you like most about church? What do you like least? How do your opinions line up with God's word?*

Relate: *I believe I can help restore the rule of God in the church simply by...*

Reforming Your Actions

If you have either a full or part-time job, pay close attention to those you work with. Ask God to show you ways you can be salt and light in the company and in the lives of individual co-workers.

ðay 29

More of the Second Sphere

Yesterday we looked at our mission to influence the family, the church, and the workplace. Today we're going to look at our call to influence education, science, and the arts.

Our Mission in the Educational System

Maybe you've seen the commercials: Knowledge is power.

Well friends, that's more than just a cute slogan. It's the truth. Those who set the educational agenda for a nation will control the future of succeeding generations.

Martin Luther argued for the Bible to be the cornerstone of a child's education:

> I advise no one to place his child where the Scriptures do not reign paramount. Every institution in which men are not constantly occupied with the Word of God must become corrupt.

Luther's words have proven prophetically accurate. If we don't restore the rule of God in our schools, who will?

Our Mission in the Scientific Community

Do you ever wonder why the people of this world seem far more concerned about the proper stewardship of our natural resources than most Christians? This is wrong. The earth and all it contains belongs to the Lord (see Psalm 24:1). The dominion mandate found in Genesis 1:26 makes us accountable to God as both producers and consumers of this treasure called earth.

When you really think about it, Christians should be the ones most interested and awed by the study of creation. We are, after all, looking at the very handiwork of God Himself! Our belief in

God as the personal Designer of the universe should position us at the forefront of the scientific community. It's time we restore the rule of God in science.

Our Mission in the Arts

Have you ever noticed that some of the cheesiest art in the world is produced by modern-day Christians? It's as if "doing it for God" makes it OK to do a mediocre job. I don't know about you, but I'm a little tired of seeing the same old religious paintings captioned by Bible verses and religious clichés.

Beginning in the first chapter of Genesis, the biblical record reveals painting, sculpting, music, architecture, crafts, poetry, psalms, and drama as evidence of the creative handiwork of God. We need a new generation of artists who understand that it is possible to be a Christian without painting religious scenes and writing indifferent fiction.

Perhaps the most notable artist in history was Bezalel, the man called by the Lord to work on the Tabernacle in Exodus 31. He was the first Spirit-filled man who was gifted, skilled, and able to teach all kinds of craftsmanship. But he did more than just produce nice art. Bezalel's art was the sacred place where a human being met the shekinah glory of God. His art was not just inspired; it was inhabited by the sovereign Creator. It was prophetic. To be spiritually inspired is to create.

It's time we restore the rule of God in the arts. Whether we're talking about music, movies, painting, architecture, dance, or a million other forms of artistic expression, each one should reflect the sovereign reign of God in the affairs of men.

Reforming Your Heart

"Slaves, obey your earthly masters with respect and fear, and with sincerity of heart, just as you would obey Christ. Obey them not only to win their favor when their eye is on you, but like slaves of Christ, doing the will of God from your heart. Serve wholeheartedly, as if you were serving the Lord, not men, because you know

that the Lord will reward everyone for whatever good he does, whether he is slave or free" (Ephesians 6:5–8, NIV).

In today's world, anyone who rules over us—teachers, bosses, coaches—could be considered masters. Using this analogy, are you a good servant ("slave")? Are you the very best student, employee, and team member you can be?

Reforming Your Mind

Reflect: *When you learn about geology, biology, or any other science, does it inspire you to glorify God? Which form of science most reminds you of the fact that God is the Creator of all things?*

Relate: *My favorite thing to study in creation is __(name something)__ because it makes me think of how God...*

Reforming Your Actions

Do you have any artistic interests such as music, dance, drawing, etc.? How can you become more skilled at what you do and learn to be truly inspired by God? Ask God to give you direction in this matter.

ðay 30

One Last Mission

We've talked about the mission that we have been given to restore the rule of God in the family, the church, the workplace, education, science, and the arts. But we probably should look at one more arena, one that has come to dominate the western world as much as the arts: sports!

Our Mission in the Sports Industry

"It was the dramatic moment the Super Bowl was always made for," reported NFL.com, "a last-second, game-winning kick. But it didn't happen until 2002, when Patriots kicker Adam Vinatieri nailed a 48-yard field goal as time expired to give New England a 20-17 win over the Rams in Super Bowl XXXVI."

Even though Super Bowl 36 didn't have the teams I wanted to see play (I actually was not a fan of either team), it had much more. It had a last-second finish that kept viewers on pins and needles until the final tick of the game clock. It had the kind of drama America always yearns for from its biggest game—complete with turnovers and long runs. Despite the worries that were prompted by the 9/11 Tragedy in New York only four months earlier, it went off without a hitch. The experts were right this time: The Superdome was the safest place in the country on that Sunday.

But more than all those things, Super Bowl XXXVI had heroes like Kurt Warner, a bold Christian who has used his position to promote godly values. Every now and then, a crowd shot would focus in on the wife of the Ram's quarterback, who was interceding fervently for her husband to win! The Rams may not have won on the field, but the Warners certainly won off the field and in the hearts of people all across America.

Thinking Biblically about Secular Issues

Although Christians historically have not done well in coliseums, they are quickly taking their place as dominant figures in the athletic industry. None too soon! Plagued by greed, drug abuse, and violence, the athletic community is in need of spiritual and moral revolution. When professional athletes can arrogantly say, "I refuse to be a role model for the youth of this nation," society should respond, "Then vacate the stadiums and arenas that are funded by taxpayer dollars."

Athletes, it's time to lead, follow, or get out of the way.

And that's exactly what Abraham Kuyper was talking about when he focused on restoring the rule of God in the seven realms of authority we've been talking about.

We will either win the culture war or lose to the forces of secular humanism, based on our responses to these issues. Although each of these realms holds the ability to influence the thoughts and actions of an entire populace, only the Church has the power to influence it for the sake of righteousness. Not only do we need Christian witness in these seven spheres, but also we must apply the appropriate biblical principles needed to sanctify the sphere itself.

If the meek shall inherit the earth, that makes the affairs of earth our business. Are we minding our own business?

Reforming Your Heart

"Blessed are the poor in spirit, For theirs is the kingdom of heaven. Blessed are those who mourn, For they shall be comforted. Blessed are the meek, For they shall inherit the earth. Blessed are those who hunger and thirst for righteousness, For they shall be filled. Blessed are the merciful, For they shall obtain mercy. Blessed are the pure in heart, For they shall see God. Blessed are the peacemakers, For they shall be called sons of God" (Matthew 5:3–9).

No matter what games you like to play—basketball, tennis, or checkers—skills can be learned with hard work and dedication. But what about your attitude? Are you the kind of person that others like to play with? Does your attitude "on the field" reflect the character of Christ?

Reforming Your Mind

Reflect: *Think seriously about this—how have you been an influence for Christ in the different areas of your life such as school, jobs, and clubs?*

Relate: *I would like to be a stronger influence for Christ in...*

Reforming Your Actions

If you are on any kind of team, athletic or academic, how much time have you spent praying for your teammates? Do that right now. Ask God to bless them and to use you to minister His love to them.

ðay 31

The Character of the Kingdom

Daniel and his friends were on the front end of seventy years worth of Babylonian captivity. In other words, they spent the rest of their lives trying to make a difference in a foreign culture. It eventually paid off. Riding the waves of change brought about by Daniel and his buddies was another key player, Nehemiah. Although he was raised in captivity, Nehemiah was inspired by men like Daniel to rise up and make a difference. Eventually he took the call seriously and returned from Babylon to rebuild the walls of Jerusalem and restore the city. The goal, of course, was the restoration of the Kingdom of God. God had promised that a son of David would one day rule God's people again, and Nehemiah was determined to do his part to help bring that promise to pass.

But despite the fact that Israel had been released from Babylonian captivity, things were never quite the same as before. For 500 years the Jews waited for the Messiah, the One who, as a son of David, would rise up, overthrow the evil empires that surrounded Israel, sit on the throne of His father, and fulfill the prophecies concerning the restoration of the Kingdom. They were seeking political redemption and were eager for vengeance. This was their vision of the restoration of the Kingdom.

But things didn't go quite as they had planned or expected.

When Jesus arrived on the scene and word began to spread that He was possibly the long-awaited Messiah, things began to get a little fuzzy. Instead of training revolutionaries and plotting the overthrow of Rome, Jesus was far more interested in the condition of men's hearts and how they lived their lives. Throughout the Gospels, His interest in the "inner" Kingdom outweighed His concern for political justice and national independence. In other words, Jesus didn't want to be president or CEO...He wanted to be Savior and Lord. That didn't sit too well with the religious leaders of Christ's day. Their ideas about the Messiah were so deeply ingrained that they considered Jesus' approach and understanding of the Kingdom to be heresy. So they killed him.

The Witness

Fast-forward to Peter's sermon on the Day of Pentecost. After a stirring speech that had everyone sitting on the edge of their seats, Peter delivered the grand finale...the oral "shot heard 'round the world."

"Therefore let all the house of Israel know assuredly that God has made this Jesus, whom you crucified, both Lord and Christ" (Acts 2:36)

.

Peter's sermon on Pentecost took 500 years of Jewish prophetic interpretation and turned it on its head. Consequently the Jewish believers had to rethink every other interpretation and expectation of the Kingdom.

Peter went on to say that Jesus was the One they had been waiting for since before the time of Nehemiah. "You just crucified the Messiah," he boldly proclaimed. "Now He has been exalted to the throne of God as your Judge."

"When they heard this, they were cut to the heart, and said to Peter and the rest of the apostles, 'Men and brethren, what shall we do?'" (Acts 2:37).

Reforming Your Heart

"For the kingdom of God is not eating and drinking, but righteousness and peace and joy in the Holy Spirit. For he who serves Christ in these things is acceptable to God and approved by men. Therefore let us pursue the things which make for peace and the things by which one may edify another" (Romans 14:17-19).

So, how do you fit into the Kingdom of God? Are you serving God in righteousness? in peace? in the joy of the Holy Spirit? If not, maybe you need to re-evaluate your idea of what the Kingdom is all about.

Reforming Your Mind

Reflect: *Do you ever find yourself wishing that God was a little more "obvious" in the way He deals with sinners? Why?*

Relate: *I know in my heart that Jesus is both Savior and Lord, but sometimes I struggle with allowing Him to truly be my (pick one: Savior/Lord) because...*

Reforming Your Actions

Read Hebrews 6:1–12. Notice the eternal weight of verse six. Can you imagine anyone drifting so far away from God's Kingdom that they could never return? What does this say to you about the nature and character of God's Kingdom? Record your thoughts in a journal or notebook.

ðay 32

A Kingdom Without Borders

Talk about a major let-down!

For centuries and generations the Jews had expected that all military power, political authority, and cultural influence would be overthrown by the zeal of the Messiah.

You have to understand the situation. Foreign governments had all but eliminated the nation of Israel. The Roman Empire—the latest of many foreign rulers—was choking the life out of the Jewish spirit. So they wanted someone who would come in, torch the place, and start over. What they got instead was a guy who had some weird ideas that threatened everything they had left. Not exactly what they had in mind.

It is easy to see how zealots radically committed to the restoration of national Israel would have been disappointed with Jesus. They lacked the patience for such small beginnings or this heart-first strategy. To say it another way, they were looking for a Delta Force war hero and got a peace-loving teacher instead. Yeah, He was the Messiah, but He was incognito and His methods were covert. The Jews didn't even recognize Him. They didn't really understand the character of the Kingdom of God, nor did they understand how the prophecies of restoration would be fulfilled. They rejected Jesus and continued to look for a messiah in the leadership mode of King David. They wanted someone who would slay the giants and take names later.

Maybe you are in the same boat. Maybe you've been somewhat disappointed or disillusioned by the church. Maybe you came to God hoping that a mighty warrior would rise up, chase all your enemies away and make life perfect. Maybe you thought that the Messiah would instantly solve all your problems while you sat back and ate grapes and read your Bible. Then you woke up...

Listen. The Kingdom of God is not about making life perfect.

You'll never know that kind of perfection as long as you live on planet earth. The Kingdom of God is about mission. Jesus never intended to complete the work with His own hands. Yes, He is the ultimate war hero, but he has anointed *you* to take His place and finish the work He started! When you accepted the grace of God to save you from sin, you also accepted the mission to become one of the many soldiers in God's army who would risk life and limb to set others free from the bondage of sin and death. This mission will be fulfilled only through the ministry of men and women of destiny who, like Daniel, commit themselves to demonstrating the character of the Kingdom in a culturally relevant manner.

The famous Methodist missionary Dr. E. Stanley Jones revealed the strategy for transforming a generation:

"For the Church to be relevant the answer is simple: Discover the Kingdom, surrender to the Kingdom, make the Kingdom your life loyalty and your life program; then in everything and everywhere you will be relevant."[1]

So, what's it gonna be? You can either accept this mission or reject it, but there can be no in-between.

Reforming Your Heart

Read Isaiah 61:1–3. It starts out like this:

"The Spirit of the Sovereign LORD is on me, because the LORD has anointed me to..."

In these verses, Isaiah describes an incredible mission: one quoted by Jesus in Luke 4:18 and passed on to you in Matthew 28:19–20.

How does it feel to know that, as a citizen of God's Kingdom, you've been called to have this kind of impact on the world?

Reforming Your Mind

Reflect: *Have you ever had the privilege of leading someone to Christ?*

Relate: *The greatest experience I've ever had in doing Isaiah 61-type stuff is...*

Reforming Your Actions

Volunteer to serve at a local soup kitchen, homeless shelter, or other outreach ministry. Do it long enough to build relationships with the hurting people of your community.

ðay 33

Beyond the Beatitudes

Once you accept the call to help usher in the Kingdom of God through relevant living, you have to get your brain around the core values of the Kingdom.

One of the biggest struggles the scribes and Pharisees had with Jesus was His teachings. The law of Moses said, for example, "Thou shall not commit adultery" (Exodus 20:14). Jesus said, "Whoever looks at a woman to lust for her has already committed adultery with her in his heart" (Matthew 5:28). Obviously the ethics of the Kingdom go far beyond the law. What matters is not just what we do to live in and advance the Kingdom, but also the attitude of our hearts beyond all we do. The teachings of Jesus and the apostles emphasize that the aim of the Gospel is to produce internal change deep within the human heart.

The Beatitudes

Take a look at Matthew 5:3–12. These Beatitudes are the very heart and soul of the Kingdom. Notice, though, that the emphasis of the Beatitudes is on character first, commitment second. Being first, doing second. Heart first, hands second.

The result of *being* someone who is poor in spirit, meek, pure in heart and so on, is that you will suffer persecution. But instead of being destroyed by it, you are strengthened by it because you are a man or woman of Kingdom character. The Beatitudes describe the essential character of Kingdom citizens and reveal the ethical conduct required of true disciples of Jesus Christ.

Beatitude seems like a really strange word, but it really just means "perfect blessedness or happiness."[1] Jesus is showing us that the one who follows these principles will be blessed of God and made to be envied by others.

Frankly, there is nothing attractive about these Beatitudes in and of themselves. It would have been much more attractive if Jesus had said, "Happy and blessed are the rich, happy, satisfied, and powerful, for theirs is a life obviously marked by Kingdom living." But He didn't. He said just the opposite. So true happiness comes when we show the world how to live by:

- Being humble even though the world idolizes arrogance and pride.
- Living a lifestyle of repentance while politicians exemplify denial and finger pointing.
- Depending on the grace of God while listening to Wall Street's attempts at self-righteousness.
- Offering mercy and grace while kids kill one another in anger and vengeance.
- Standing for truth, justice, and peace even though most of the religious folks are apathetic and complacent.

What society is looking for is the power of transformed lives. What they need are true spiritual war heroes who will risk it all to help set them free from a life of hopelessness and dead-end streets. They need people who have discovered and are living true happiness.

You may say you believe in the royal law of love, but are you living it? You may applaud purity and holiness, but are you demonstrating them? You may profess faithfulness to God, but are you sacrificially giving?

The new birth is not simply a ticket to heaven; it is a change of governments. The Beatitudes deal with the reign of the Lord Jesus Christ in the deepest parts of our heart. Does the Kingdom reign in you?

Reforming Your Heart

"But when the time had fully come, God sent his Son, born of a woman, born under law, to redeem those under law, that we might receive the full rights of sons. Because you are sons, God sent the Spirit of his Son into our hearts, the Spirit who calls out, 'Abba, Father.' So you are no longer a slave, but a son; and since you are a

son, God has made you also an heir" (Galatians 4:4-7, NIV).

We've talked a lot about being Kingdom citizens and about the nature of God's Kingdom as it is fleshed out in our lives. But we are more than citizens: We are heirs! Sons and daughters of the King Himself! Do you feel like a child of the King?

Reforming Your Mind

Reflect: *Look again at the Beatitudes. Which one do you struggle with the most?*

Relate: *The Beatitude that is most unlike me is   (name one)   because...*

Reforming Your Actions

Pray this confessional prayer: Pray with your heart, not your head. Lord, I know that the Kingdom belongs to the poor in spirit. I know, too, that I am a sinner, that I am defenseless and that I am in desperate need of your grace and mercy. I have absolutely no hope of salvation without Jesus Christ. Spiritually, I am bankrupt, completely empty, totally unqualified to commune with You. All my abilities are actually liabilities before You. I will never be able to pay the price for salvation. Instead, I am forced to rely on Christ to "foot the bill." Thank You, Father, for the work of your Son. Thank You for allowing me to enter into the Kingdom of heaven! Amen.

ðay 34

How Do We Establish the Kingdom?

If nothing else, the Beatitudes should have made it clear that establishing the Kingdom of God involves more than preaching the Gospel. So, where do we begin the process of transforming our culture? What can we do to become agents of change in the lives of those around us?

Earning the Right to Be Heard

Before we will ever influence the heart of a generation, we must first earn the right to be heard. This is why the lifestyle of believers is so important: People are watching us. They connect our beliefs with our actions. And this is the way it should be.

"Let your light so shine before men, that they may see your good works and glorify your Father in heaven" (Matthew 5:16).

When Jesus walked the earth, He did some pretty miraculous things. His fame spread throughout the country faster than an e-mail virus posing as photos of some hot teen superstar. But I have always been fascinated by a simple statement made about those who were watching Christ with skeptical eyes:

"When Jesus had finished saying these things, the crowds were amazed at his teaching, because he taught as one who had authority, and not as their teachers of the law" (Matthew 7:28–29, NIV).

The teachers of the law were the official authorities of Jesus' day, yet they had no authority in the eyes of the people. They were hypocrites. Posers. Oblivious to the disconnect between their words and their actions. They had lost all respect in the eyes of the crowds. The people were cynical and skeptical of religion. Sounds a lot like people today.

Then Jesus steps onto the scene. His words match His lifestyle. He is passionate, persistent, and driven by a force that is unlike anything the crowds have ever witnessed. His words carry the weight of an authority, yet He holds no office. And the people are amazed.

Through character, Jesus earned the right to be heard. He didn't need a badge, a bodyguard, a band, or a book deal to validate His life and ministry.

The same is true for you and me. If you want the skeptics to hear the good news, earn the right to be heard by having a lifestyle that backs up your beliefs. Participate in Christian organizations, such as local churches, parachurch ministries, and world missions. Look for opportunities to express the value system of the Kingdom in whatever career you desire: science, the arts, media, industry, politics, economics, or education.

When Christians advance into every sphere of society, exemplifying the character of the Kingdom, we show the world that there is a better way of living. The Kingdom offers us the opportunity to succeed in life without following the same rules by which the Babylonians play.

Reforming Your Heart

"So whether you eat or drink or whatever you do, do it all for the glory of God. Do not cause anyone to stumble, whether Jews, Greeks or the church of God—even as I try to please everybody in every way. For I am not seeking my own good but the good of many, so that they may be saved. Follow my example, as I follow the example of Christ" (1 Corinthians 10:31-11:1, NIV).

Can you say that to your friends? Is your life committed enough (notice I didn't say "perfect") that you can urge others to follow your example? Does the character of your relationship with God qualify you to speak as an authority on the subject of Christ?

Reforming Your Mind

Reflect: *What is the one area in which you would be most comfortable in asking others to follow your example?*

Relate: *The one area of my life in which I would most like to improve my commitment level is...*

Reforming Your Actions

Come up with a signal of some sort that you and your accountability partner can use to privately warn one another when you see each other stepping "out of character" as a Kingdom citizen and heir.

ðay 35

Serving God by Influencing the State

Throughout history there have been scores of leaders who have all given in to the temptation to establish a physical Christian empire.

You may be saying, "But isn't that a good thing? Shouldn't we want to live in an official Christian nation?" A brief look at the "church" when Jesus arrived on the scene should answer that question. Or a glance at the church when Rome was ruled by a papal government. Or a glance at the fundamentalist Islamic states that exist in the world. When religion is the government, liberty is crushed and justice is silenced. In such a state, faith and righteousness are mandated by rule of law, and enforced with severe penalties. And whenever we assume that righteousness is established in a culture by the courtrooms, then we are to some degree advocating the same outcome.

Our hope does not lie in political redemption. It never has and it never will. This was the mistake that Israel made and the reason they didn't recognize the Messiah when he arrived.

Please don't misunderstand. We do need to pass righteous laws and elect moral leadership at every level of society. But we must continually remind ourselves, and those around us, that the Kingdom of God is established by Jesus' lordship in the hearts of people. Laws against unrighteousness are only bandaids for what ails us. What we really need are men and women who will humble themselves, pray, and work *within the culture* for another spiritual awakening. Culture must be changed from the inside out, not by laws imposed from the outside in.

Besides, God has not called everyone to be involved in the political arena. As far as we know, Daniel—a remarkable leader who served faithfully in Babylon under the very kings who opposed his nation, oppressed his people, and decimated his culture—was the only Jewish prophet to spend his entire ministry working as a public servant for a heathen empire. He successfully served three foreign kings and two pagan governments in a career that lasted seventy years.

Daniel demonstrated the character of the Kingdom even when he could easily have betrayed the Babylonians and brought them down. (During the seven years when Nebuchadnezzar was out of his mind, who do you suppose was running his kingdom?) This servant leader refused to compromise his integrity even when surrounded by rotten politicians, New Age charlatans, and perverse pagans. The fact that Daniel maintained a lifelong reputation for unimpeachable integrity and unswerving commitment to the Lord makes him an important model for Christians in the twenty-first century.

Daniel and his Hebrew companions lived, as Jesus did, in the presence of sin, as servants to unrighteous men, without allowing the presence of sin to overwhelm them. In the end, the influence of the Kingdom won out. If you are faithful and walk in the character of the Kingdom, it will for you, too. It's time for Christians to take seriously the call to be *in the world*, but not *of* the world.

Reforming Your Heart

"[God] also made us sufficient as ministers of a new covenant—not of the letter but of the Spirit; for the letter kills, but the Spirit gives life" (2 Corinthians 3:6).

Which is easier, making up laws that force people to do he right thing or investing in their lives and helping them learn to do the right thing because they want to do the right thing?

Reforming Your Mind

Reflect: *Do you feel "sufficient" (or competent) as a minister of the new covenant? Do you feel comfortable sharing the life-giving Spirit of God's Word with those in need? Why?*

Relate: *I've had first-hand experience with the crushing power of the "letter of the law." (Share your story. Tell how things would have gone much better if your "punisher" had been more concerned about your heart than your actions.)*

Reforming Your Actions

What unwritten law do you most often enforce on others? Think of three things you can do differently that will allow you to minister to people instead of pass judgement on them.

ðay 36

Five Components of Reformation

More than ever before, it seems, Christians and non-Christians alike have come to believe that global transformation is possible in our generation. People genuinely want to make a difference. But the haunting question remains: How?

The net-age has turned the average citizen into an expert with a global platform. Every person with a computer has a theory about what's wrong with the world and how to fix things. But no man-made theory will ever come close to solving the world's problems. For challenges that big, we have to turn off the computer and open up the only source for timeless wisdom—the Word of God.

Jeremiah 29 reveals five components of biblical reformation in a nation. Originally written to the captives of Nebuchadnezzar, these principles are just as relevant to our own cultural crisis. If we'll listen, God's Word can help us awaken the sleeping morality of any nation. Today we'll take a look at Jeremiah's first component of reformation.

1. We Must Acknowledge and Honor Spiritual Authority.

"These are the words of the letter that Jeremiah the prophet sent from Jerusalem to the remainder of the elders who were carried away captive—to the priests, the prophets, and all the people whom Nebuchadnezzar had carried away captive from Jerusalem to Babylon" (Jeremiah 29:1–2).

It's Friday night and you just found out about a last-minute party at your best friend's house. Normally, it would not have been a big deal, but this Friday you had already promised to take your little brother (or sister) and a few friends to the mall.

Determined to work out this situation so everybody wins, you put your brain to work and come up with the perfect solution. You rehearse your presentation and go boldly before your little brother, hoping for a decision in your favor.

Whoa! Back up this train. Did I just say you go before your *little brother*? A thousand pardons. Any idiot knows that in a situation this volatile you go straight to the decision-makers and bypass the little guys. When you want a situation to change in your favor, you go to the ones in authority to help. That's exactly what Jeremiah did.

Jeremiah's first step was to address those who sat in the seat of authority in society. Jeremiah was acknowledging the principles of submission and authority. He understood that if you turn the head, you turn the body.

The same principle was at work throughout the three-and-a-half-year ministry of Jesus. Have you ever wondered why He spent so much time addressing the Pharisees of the day? After all, they were—in many ways—the adversaries who were trying to kill Him. However, Jesus knew that as spiritual gatekeepers, the scribes and Pharisees possessed the authority to open the door to revival, restoration, and reformation—or to close it for the whole generation.

If we want to see reformation in our generation, the first thing we must do is figure out who the "gatekeepers" are in our communities and country. And then we need to pray for them as if our lives depended on it. Some day they might.

Reforming Your Heart

"I urge, then, first of all, that requests, prayers, intercession and thanksgiving be made for everyone—for kings and all those in authority, that we may live peaceful and quiet lives in all godliness and holiness. This is good, and pleases God our Savior, who wants all men to be saved and to come to a knowledge of the truth" (1 Timothy 2:1–4, NIV).

It's easy to criticize leaders and politicians as being immoral or incompetent. But part of the responsibility for our leaders' lack of character or competence should fall on our shoulders: If we would spend more time interceding for them instead of talking about them, they would be changed by the mighty hand of God! So, are you praying for your leaders?

Reforming Your Mind

Reflect: *When is the last time you prayed earnestly for your president, principal, and parents?*

Relate: *The leader in my life that I am most frustrated with is _____ and the last time I prayed for him/her was _____.*

Reforming Your Actions

Make a list of at least three leaders in your life who seem to be in desperate need of your prayers. Think especially about those who are not Christians. Spend the next thirty minutes praying for them. For political leaders, use the internet to do research on this person so you can make your prayers more specific.

Ɗay 37

A Day of Remembrance

Yesterday we looked at the first component of spiritual reformation according to Jeremiah: addressing and interceding for the spiritual gatekeepers. Figure out who's really in charge and then ask God to bless them and to give you favor in their eyes.

The second component of reformation is one, which *should* come easily, but is so often overlooked.

2. We Must Keep the Past in Perspective.

"Thus says the LORD of hosts, the God of Israel, to all who were carried away captive, whom I have caused to be carried away from Jerusalem to Babylon" (Jeremiah 29:4).

Anticipating Judah's tendency toward finger-pointing, Jeremiah began his instructions by reminding her of the reason for her captivity. "Don't forget who orchestrated these events," he said. Jeremiah knew that by reminding the exiles of the One who had caused their captivity, he was reminding them of the reason for their captivity. This was his attempt to reconnect them with their history, in order to position them for their destiny.

Americans should be very adept at remembering. We have a national holiday nearly every month that was originally designed as a way of reminding us of some great event in our history. Unfortunately, we've turned most of these holidays into just one more reason to get out of school (or work), spend money, and indulge in some pursuit of pleasure. Rarely ever does a holiday get celebrated as a day of remembrance.

That's a real shame, too. To forget the past is to repeat it.

If we want to see spiritual and social reformation in our nation, we need to be reminded of the character of the men and women who set sail in search of religious liberty; of the biblical foundations on which our nation was built; of the purpose behind its formation; of the biblical content found in our documents of freedom; of the price that was paid to ensure our freedom; even of the failures of our nation over the last two centuries.

To forget the past is to abort the future.

There's a great book that came out a number of years ago called *The Fourth Turning: An American Prophecy.* In this book, authors William Strauss and Neil Howe take the reader on a tour of history. They say (quite convincingly), that history does not move along a straight line. Instead, it moves along a giant circle, repeating itself every 100 years or so. Unfortunately, the lessons we should have learned from mistakes made a century ago get repeated. Of course, this is really nothing new. Israel went through the same endlessly repeating cycle during the period known as "Judges" in the Old Testament. Makes you wonder what would happen if we'd become better at remembering.

There is power in the act of righteous remembering. We must remind ourselves that we are connected with something much bigger than ourselves. God's purpose predates our personal perspective. This thing did not begin with us. We are joined with a great cloud of witnesses.

It's time we got serious about learning to respect history and see the bigger picture. If we don't, we could be leading ourselves on a destructive path toward the sins of the past.

Reforming Your Heart

"They refused to listen and failed to remember the miracles you performed among them. They became stiff-necked and in their rebellion appointed a leader in order to return to their slavery. But you are a forgiving God, gracious and compassionate, slow to anger and abounding in love" (Nehemiah 9:17, NIV).

How did you celebrate Christmas last year? Was it truly a time of reflecting on the birth of your Savior? How about Easter? the

Fourth of July? Thanksgiving? Do you regularly reflect on the wonders of God at work in your life and country? Do you mourn over the sins of the past and pray for God to deliver you from the potential of repeating them in the future?

Reforming Your Mind

Reflect: *What is your favorite holiday? Why? What could you do in your own celebrations to restore the true meaning of that holiday?*

Relate: *The holiday that I have misused the most is...*

Reforming Your Actions

Together with your accountability partner, plan a special day of remembrance for the next national holiday on the calendar. Go to your local library and learn as much as you can about the origins of the holiday. Invite your friends and family members to share with you in this act of remembering in a way that glorifies God and celebrates righteousness.

Ðay 38

Money with a Mission

O K, we've established the fact that we need to work with authorities and remember the past. So what's next on the road to reformation?

3. We Must Become Financially Stable.
"Thus says the LORD of hosts...Build houses and dwell in them; plant gardens and eat their fruit" (Jeremiah 29:4–5).

You can imagine the shock that must have registered in the hearts of these captives, on hearing Jeremiah's instructions. The prophet actually expected them to put down roots in this foreign land!

No doubt about it, there's a lot of moving around these days. Although moving is still a pain, it is a hundred times easier than it was in the early days of our nation's history. Because it is so easy to start over, it's rare to find people who have truly committed themselves to making a difference in a particular community. Then there are people like Bob Beckett, a pastor who has committed himself for life to his church and city:

"Think about [Jeremiah 29] in light of making your own territorial commitment. The children of Israel hardly considered Babylon their home. They longed for the day they could return to Jerusalem to get on with their lives. But God was telling them through the prophet Jeremiah to live their lives fully in the place where He had brought them. He was reminding them that He was the One who had put them there, and while they remained, they were to get on with the business of living life and blessing the land."[1]

The entire theology of the Israelites revolved around a promise that God had given to Abraham as the father of the nation. Among the many incredible things that God had established as part of his covenant promise to Abraham was this: "And you shall be a blessing" (Genesis 12:2).

Are you a blessing to your community? Are you giving more than you are taking? That may seem like an odd question, especially for those of you who don't work or who only have part-time jobs flipping burgers. But the covenant of God with His people is that you *will* be a blessing to your community.

Listen to Deuteronomy 8:18: "And you shall remember the LORD your God, for it is He who gives you power to get wealth, that He may establish His covenant which He swore to your fathers, as it is this day."

It is God who gives you the ability to make money. You may be making hundreds of dollars a week or you may be making only a few. Either way, your increase comes from the hand of God. Part of His plan for giving you money is so you can be a blessing to your community. By doing so, you are positioning yourself in a way that God can confirm His covenant: You will be a blessing!

Bless the people in your community and let God use you to reach those people with the good news that God loves them.

Reforming Your Heart

"While they were listening to this, he went on to tell them a parable, because he was near Jerusalem and the people thought that the kingdom of God was going to appear at once. He said: 'A man of noble birth went to a distant country to have himself appointed king and then to return. So he called ten of his servants and gave them ten minas. 'Put this money to work,' he said, 'until I come back'" (Luke 19:11–13, NIV).

Do you realize that everything you have belongs to God? Every penny you earn belongs to God. If this bothers you, then He isn't really Lord of your life. But if He is Lord, then you realize that you are simply a steward of His resources. Put His money to work in your community. Use it as a way to reach others with the Gospel. Be a blessing.

Reforming Your Mind

Reflect: *Are there any stores at which you regularly shop? If so, how can you begin building relationships with the owner and employees in order to share with them the good news?*

Relate: *I would really like to be a blessing to the people who work at _____. Will you pray for me, that God will give me favor with them?*

Reforming Your Actions

Visit your favorite store today. Strike up a conversation with the employees or owner. Learn their names and faces and begin praying for them.

ðay 39

Building Strong Families

We've been looking at Jeremiah 29 for the five components of cultural reformation. So far we've talked about authority, remembering, and blessing. Today we're gonna get personal, so buckle up!

4. We Must Help Build Strong Families.

"Take wives and beget sons and daughters; and take wives for your sons and give your daughters to husbands, so that they may bear sons and daughters—that you may be increased there, and not diminished" (Jeremiah 29:6).

As if Jeremiah hadn't already ruffled enough feathers, in verse six he really crossed the line. Just think about the startling implications that are found here! Jeremiah said, "Even though you're captives in a strange land, one that doesn't embrace your value system, unpack your bags. Get married. Buy houses. Plant gardens. Raise children. And change your generation."

You've got to be kidding! God couldn't possibly expect His people to go about life as if everything were hunky-dory. Look where they were. They were slaves, for Pete's sake! They should've been coming up with a plan of escape, not starting families. That's when you stop and realize that God has a tendency to require things of us that oftentimes seem backwards, even counter-productive at first glance.

Jeremiah knew that, rather than contributing to the problem, those unborn generations were, in fact, the solution to the problem. With six decades of captivity remaining before them, those exiles had been prophetically positioned by God to reclaim the cultural landscape through multigenerational ministry.

For some reason, the purpose of God usually takes at least three generations to implement. In other words it takes multiple generations. Don't ask me why, that's just the way it is. Maybe it has something to do with the whole cycle-of-history thing (four generations representing one cycle).

Of course, our enemy—Satan—is equally aware of this trend and eagerly attempts to impede the progress of the Kingdom through generational disconnection. By alienating fathers from sons and mothers from daughters, he has been able to destroy continuity among the generations.

So here's the kicker, the up-close-and-personal stuff: How's it going with you and your parents?

The strategy for world dominion has always flowed out of a home environment. If the enemy can succeed in destroying your relationship with your family (or at the very least make it sour), then he wins. He knows that you can't reform the culture without the help of those before you and after you. Never has there been a greater need for society to renew its commitment to family than there is today. Your future depends on it.

Let me say a word to the girls who, despite ridicule from your friends, really just want to be stay-at-home moms. The world would make you feel as though you cannot make a difference in the community because you are focused on bottles, diapers, and runny noses. But remember, the hand that rocks the cradle rules the world. Thank God for Kingdom Moms who have raised us the righteous way as painful as that may have been!

Reforming Your Heart

"Children, obey your parents in the Lord, for this is right. 'Honor your father and mother,' which is the first commandment with a promise:' that it may be well with you and you may live long on the earth'" (Ephesians 6:1-3).

When you were a kid, your parents were your heroes. You weren't ashamed to be with them or even to show them affection in public.

You were proud of them. What happened? What better way is there to "honor" your parents than to show the world that you love them and are proud of them?

Reforming Your Mind

Reflect: *How's it going with you and your parents? Is your relationship with them what it should be? What are you going to do about it?*

Relate: *The things I admire most about my parents are...*

Reforming Your Actions

The next time you are in a public place with your parents (especially in front of their or your friends), give them a big hug or kiss and let them know you love them. Then, after they get up from the floor (where they fainted in shock), assure them that you aren't buttering them up—you just wanted them to know that you still think they're awesome.

ðay 40

Influence 101

Somebody give me a big drum roll here…This is it, the final component of the plan for global domination laid out by Jeremiah as he was inspired by God.

5. We Must Take Social Responsibility.

"Seek the peace of the city where I have caused you to be carried away captive, and pray to the LORD for it; for in its peace you will have peace" (Jeremiah 29:7).

This is what you call a scriptural paradox. As difficult as it is to face, the Lord says we find our peace in the peace of the city. Let that thought sink in for a moment: Even though our peace is not contingent on world conditions, it is connected to the peace of the city.

Wow! Heavy!

When the city is blessed, the people rejoice. When my neighbors rejoice, I have cause to rejoice with them. My concerns are set at peace.

Think about that. The "natural" things that eat away at our peace—crime, poverty, broken relationships, etc.—if absent (or at least reduced), make life better for all of us! So if I can do things to help reduce crime, provide for the poor and mend broken relationships (among others), I am contributing to the peace of the city, and also to my own peace! It's a win-win situation!

We must learn to take responsibility in our schools, neighborhoods, and workplaces. We need to see it as our God-ordained call to be peacemakers. Jesus said, "Blessed are the peacemakers, for they shall be called sons of God" (Matthew 5:9).

In addition to the five components of reformation found in Jeremiah 29, chapter 28 lists two other important items that we have to get our brains around.

We Must Recover Spiritual and Biblical Integrity

Jeremiah had a tough job: He had to prophesy to people who had been snatched from their homes and turned into slaves. It was not a happy time. Not only were the people in despair of their captivity, but another prophet, Hananiah, had arisen to prophesy immediate deliverance. But God had a different perspective. Because of their rebellion, He had actually caused Israel to be carried away into captivity. It was the law of sowing and reaping. God did not intend to deliver them for seventy more years.

If we are to live as a prophetic people, we must be willing to say what God says, even when it goes against the tide of public opinion. That's what Jeremiah did.

Then the prophet Jeremiah said to Hananiah the prophet, "Hear now, Hananiah, the LORD has not sent you, but you make this people trust in a lie" (Jeremiah 2815).

As we seek to tune our ears to the frequency of heaven, we must remind ourselves that scripture takes precedence over every spiritual gift given to the Church.

Reforming Your Heart

"As he approached Jerusalem and saw the city, he wept over it and said, 'If you, even you, had only known on this day what would bring you peace—but now it is hidden from your eyes. The days will come upon you when your enemies will build an embankment against you and encircle you and hem you in on every side. They will dash you to the ground, you and the children within your walls. They will not leave one stone on another, because you did not recognize the time of God's coming to you'" (Luke 19:41–44, NIV).

Do you weep over the sin of those in your school, community, and city? Is your heart broken when you think of those that are blinded by sin? Do you have the "heart of God" for your neighborhood?

Reforming Your Mind

Reflect: *Crime, poverty, broken relationships...do you consider it your responsibility to work toward healing those wounds in your community? Why?*

Relate: *The "need" in our community that touches me the most is...*

Reforming Your Actions

Talk with leaders in your community about the specific needs of people in your neighborhood and school. Ask God to give you a plan for making a difference.

Ðay 41

Building Fences or Bridges?

Just when you think you have it all together, God does something to bring you down to reality. Several years ago I set out on a journey that could not have been more religiously awkward. I felt like Peter sitting on the housetop in Joppa, totally confused by the leading of the Lord.

I suppose I should not have been confused. It was a simple plan: personally infiltrate popular culture; go to people where they are, and become an honest but unconditional friend of sinners. In other words (and here is the radical concept), do what Jesus did!

Even preachers have been known to struggle with the basics sometimes!

As odd as it sounds, Christians have a lot of ideas and practices that tend to isolate us from the world and make us irrelevant to the average Joe. I had these obstacles to overcome, too—my background and religious heritage. Let me explain.

I cannot remember a time when I did not want to preach. When asked at three years of age, "What do you want to be when you grow up?", I replied, "A preacher of the Gospel and a game warden!" (How's that for diversity?) I succeeded at the first goal, sort of.

I spent the early years of my ministry building fences—between the Church and the world, between my church and other churches, between my denomination and other denominations, between the pastors and the people. We're not talking pretty little picket fences. I built my fences high and solid, constructing them with scriptures taken out of context and biblical principles misapplied to support my personal views. I guess you could say I had lots of zeal, but very little wisdom. I tried to reach out to my unsaved classmates, but I kept hitting the wall—the wall that I had built! My religious restrictions made it difficult for me to relate to them on any level deeper than casual friendship. My frustration began to mount. How could I reach my unsaved schoolmates if I could scarcely communicate with them?

My frustration came to a head in my first year of pastoring. I realized that I been taught to build fences and was instead harboring a secret longing to build bridges.

In one defining moment, I cried out, "God, I'm tired of building fences. Make me a bridge-builder!"

The following month I quit my job as a fence-building "pastor" and set out to discover the place where God was moving me.

I felt alive for the very first time.

Twelve years later, a man directed a message to me: "God has heard the cry of your heart and has chosen to make you a bridge. You will experience the discomfort of having people walk over your life in order to enter into their promised land, but the reward will be well worth the price you have to pay."

That message provided the confidence I needed to leave the old ways behind and step out into God's plan for my life. Since then, I have been slowly learning to speak the language of Babylon, but it hasn't been easy.

Reforming Your Heart

"For Christ's love compels us, because we are convinced that one died for all, and therefore all died. And he died for al, that those who live should no longer live for themselves, but for him who died for them and was raised again. So from now on we regard no one from a worldly point of view. Though we once regarded Christ in this way, we do so no longer. Therefore, if anyone is in Christ, he is a new creation; the old has gone, the new has come! All this is from God, who reconciled us to himself through Christ and gave us the ministry of reconciliation: that God was reconciling the world to himself in Christ, not counting men's sins against them. And he has committed to us the message of reconciliation. We are therefore Christ's ambassadors, as though God were making his appeal through us. We implore you on Christ's behalf: Be reconciled to

God" (2 Corinthians 5:14–20, NIV).

What is Paul describing here: Fence-building or bridge-building? Of the two approaches to Christianity, which is more like you?

Reforming Your Mind

Reflect: *If I were to take a poll at school, would your friends say that you are more of a fence-builder or a bridge-builder?*

Relate: *The biggest wall that I have built is the one between _____. (Example: between my church and other churches; between rich and poor, etc.)*

Reforming Your Actions

What can you do to change the way you relate to the non-Christians in your school or community? What changes can you make in your own life that will help you to become a more effective "minister of reconciliation"?

ðay 42

The Adventure Begins

So now you know that God had every intention of messing up my nice, neat little fenced-in world that I had built. He had a journey for me that would prove…uh, exciting, to say the least!

It began with a visit to the doctor's office.

"You've got to do something to relieve some of this stress," the doctor said. "If you don't find an outlet, the pressure is going to kill you. Have you thought about golf?"

Almost as an afterthought, the doctor asked, "Was there anything you really liked to do when you were a kid?"

Church was what I did growing up. There were simply not many other options. The only other activity that fueled my fire, apart from ministry, was having a pack on my back, a hunting rifle under my arm and a night out under the stars.

"Well, that's it!" the doctor cried as if he had discovered the cure for cancer. "Have you ever hunted with a bow and arrow? I think you need to take up archery. It's a year-round sport."

Which is how I became a bow hunter.

There is, however, an aspect of bow hunting that I had not anticipated: other bow hunters.

They are, by and large, a pretty rugged bunch. It didn't take long to figure out that I was way out of my comfort zone.

The initial pressure I felt to share the Gospel with those guys was probably motivated more by religious obligation than by genuine concern for their souls. For a pastor with few non-Christian friends in his life, I was learning to relate the hard way—and discovering a lot in the process.

A Stunning Discovery

Let me tell you a secret about pastors, if you have not already figured this out. Most of us preach from the pulpit about things we are going through ourselves.

One Sunday morning, I got an inspired whim.

"How many of you here this morning have five unsaved friends, unsaved people with whom you have a meaningful relationship? If you do, raise your hand."

Silence. Perfect stillness. It was a twilight zone moment.

I figured they had not understood, or else I had been mistaken and they were not paying attention. I repeated my question.

Still no response.

"How about three?" I asked.

Nothing.

"Two? How about one?"

As I stood before the congregation, the reality of our cultural retreat hit me like a ton of bricks. I was forced to face the fact that most of our church growth was from church-hoppers, not new Christians.

We had some decisions to make. We could hide out in our Christian caves and hang on till the end, thus sealing our fate as an irrelevant subculture. (I knew all about that option.) Or we could get sucked up into the "foreign" culture, and lose our identity, beliefs, and values. Or we could infiltrate and infect the culture with what we had—the good news.

The challenge to my church, and to me as one of its members, was to become culturally relevant infiltrators, with no questions or second thoughts about our identity in Christ, who carried that confidence with us into the mainstream of postmodern culture.

Reforming Your Heart

"And a voice came to him, 'Rise, Peter; kill and eat'" (Acts 10:13).

Read Acts 10, the entire chapter.

Why was Peter initially offended by the "vision" he had? Are there any "unclean" people in your schools or neighborhood to whom God is asking you to reach out? God was asking Peter to "consume" the Gentiles, not to be consumed by them. What's the difference?

Reforming Your Mind

Reflect: *How many non-Christian friends do you have? Are you consuming or being consumed?*

Relate: *There is one special person I would really like to have the privilege of leading to Christ and helping to grow in Christ. Name the person and tell why you have a burden for him/her.*

Reforming Your Actions

If you cannot name at least one friend whose life you are influencing for Christ, make a list of at least three ways you could begin building relationships with others. For example, you may want to join a club, sign up for an athletic team, or volunteer at a local outreach.

ðay 43

How to Win Friends

The goal of discipleship is to become like the teacher. Perhaps one of the surest signs of a true disciple of Christ is that person's ability to submit to Him without compromise, while at the same time being a genuine friend of sinners. Of course, this is no easy task. To love the Lord without compromise while being a genuine friend of sinners requires at least four things.

1. You Must Know Who You Are in Christ.

Many Christians are afraid to develop meaningful relationships with non-Christians because they do not understand the security of their own personal relationship with Jesus Christ

Part of what makes reaching out so tough is that we all have a built-in desire to be loved and cared for by others. So when we try to be a genuine friend of sinners, we wind up being controlled by our desire to be accepted by sinners. For teenagers, this natural and God-given desire for love and acceptance (like *other* natural and God-given desires) is often in overdrive. The key is to learn how to discipline those desires. Our desire and need to be loved simply cannot (and must not) be met in a relationship with non-Christians. If that happens, we become adulterers and adulteresses. Those needs are the ones that God Himself wants to meet…and He's a pretty jealous God! To be a friend of sinners in the way that Jesus was a friend of sinners means that we go into the relationship knowing that, for the most part, it's going to be one-way. And it takes true confidence in God and His word to do that.

It's *good* to be a friend to those who miss the mark (sinners). But it's *bad* to need their love and approval so much that we conform to their values and worldviews. It's also *bad* to be so unsure of God's love for us—and our love for Him—that we refuse to take the risk of reaching out for fear of being "re-infected" with sin.

2. They Refuse to Be Confined by Cultural Barriers.

If Jesus had consulted a public relations expert about choosing His inner circle, He would have been told that Matthew was the least desirable of all possible candidates. Yet Jesus did not simply approve Matthew's application; He sought him out.

Have you ever noticed that it is the non-Christian community, for the most part, and not the Christian community, calling for the separation of church and state? There is something deep inside of each of us that *knows* it is impossible to serve two masters. Your non-Christian friends will try to shut you out, but not because they are rejecting Christianity. Instead, they are trying to *protect* their relationship with sin. So the key to infiltrating the culture—to breaking past those natural barriers—is to build strong personal friendships with those you are trying to reach. Once you've crossed those invisible barriers by offering genuine care and concern, they will be much more likely to want what you have—a life-changing relationship with Christ!

Reforming Your Heart

"As it is written: 'For your sake we face death all day long; we are considered as sheep to be slaughtered.' No, in all these things we are more than conquerors through him who loved us. For I am convinced that neither death nor life, neither angels nor demons, neither the present nor the future, nor any powers, neither height nor depth, nor anything else in all creation, will be able to separate us from the love of God that is in Christ Jesus our Lord" (Romans 8:36–39, NIV).

Think about a herd of sheep being raised in a slaughterhouse all for the purpose of becoming food and clothing for someone. Do you think the sheep get anything whatsoever out of that relationship? How is being a friend of sinners like being a "sheep to be slaughtered"?

Reforming Your Mind

Reflect: *Have you ever found yourself in a situation where you wound up being influenced by non-Christian friends instead of being the influencer?*

Relate: *I want to be a friend of sinners and make a difference in people's lives, but I struggle with...*

Reforming Your Actions

Do you struggle with doubts about your relationship with Christ? Would you like to be more confident in Christ? Spend some time looking up the following passages of Scripture as a way of discovering who you are in Christ:

Matthew 5:13–14; John 1:12; 15:1, 5, 15, 16;Acts 1:8; Romans 5:1; 8:1, 2, 28, 31–39; 1 Corinthians 3:16; 6:17, 19, 20; 12:27; 2 Corinthians 1:21, 22; 5:17–21; 6:1; Ephesians 1:1, 5; 2:6, 10, 18; 3:12; Philippians 1:6; 3:20; 4:13; Colossians 1:14; 2:10; 3:3; 2 Timothy 1:7; Hebrews 4:16; 1 John 5:18;

Ðay 44

How to Win More Friends

Yesterday we talked about two things that are necessary in order to be known as people who love the Lord without compromise while being a genuine friend of sinners: knowing who you are in Christ and crossing cultural barriers. Let's look at two more characteristics of postmodern soulwinners.

3. They Are Unashamed of Their Love for Others.

The Pharisees were the religious conservatives and fundamentalists of their day. They took great pride in how strictly they observed the Law. You could say they "majored in sacrifice," but they certainly flunked in compassion. In fact, many of them hated the gentiles and "common" Jews.

Seem strange? Not really. We like to say that we "love the sinner, hate the sin," but the reality is that we hate the sinner, too. Those people who make fun of Christians and do everything they can to make life miserable for believers...can you honestly say that you care about them?

You see, wearing the latest designer clothing, listening to the hottest bands, and knowing the language and cultural fads and faux-pas will not communicate the Gospel to secular people. Speaking the language and knowing the customs of contemporary culture are nothing more than vehicles for communicating across the great divide called *sin*. But it is the unashamed love of Christ that builds the bridge to unbelievers. Once you have the bridge of love and a culturally savvy vehicle, you can begin transporting the truth of the gospel. But I can't say it enough: It all starts with genuine love.

Paul commented that a great sacrifice, a generous gift or a dynamic message without love is like a noisy gong and tinkling cymbal. Pure love, by contrast, is able to bridge any gap—even the massive gaps between generations, cultures and languages.

4. They Practice the Ministry of Reconciliation.

If you've never seen the movie *The Mission*, you need to see it. The opening scene is really powerful. A Jesuit missionary sent to reach an isolated tribe in South America had been crucified by the very people he was trying to reach. Imitating the crucifix that hung on a chain around his neck, they tied his body to a cross and sent it washing down over a huge waterfall. Soon afterward his body washed up on the bank of the river where his companions were camped. Wasting no time in grieving, they buried the body of their slain companion and sent another member of the Jesuit order to minister to the tribe.

The only way to reach them, however, was to climb straight up the craggy face of the waterfall over which the murdered priest has just come crashing down. After hours of relentless climbing, the second priest barely managed to reach the top, where he entered the jungle. Knowing the tribe's love of music, he reached into his water-soaked pouch, pulled out a reed flute and began to play. Risking his very life, this missionary entered their world.

That is what it means to be a minister of reconciliation: laying down your own life in order to help someone else have a first-hand experience with the love of God!

Reforming Your Heart

"And the Lord's servant must not quarrel; instead, he must be kind to everyone, able to teach, not resentful. Those who oppose him he must gently instruct, in the hope that God will grant them repentance leading them to a knowledge of the truth, and that they will come to their senses and escape from the trap of the devil, who has taken them captive to do his will" (2 Timothy 2:24–26, NIV).

When someone opposes your beliefs or your way of life—passively (by simply shrugging it off) or aggressively (by telling you off), how do you respond? Does love continue to be the bridge over which you travel, or do you back up to your side and start tossing truth grenades?

Reforming Your Mind

Reflect: *If you were put on trial for attempting to love sinners, would you be convicted? What evidence would be cited against you?*

Relate: *Talk about someone who has "opposed" your beliefs or way of life and how you responded. What would you do differently if faced with the same situation today?*

Reforming Your Actions

Get together with your accountability partner and a few other friends. Visit your local video store, rent *The Mission,* and watch it together. Afterwards, talk about the faith, love, and commitment of the missionaries.

ðay 45

How Much Do You Love?

Do you want to begin reaching out to your non-Christian friends and acquaintances? If so, then you have to be thoughtful and strategic. The one-size-fits-all strategy of door-to-door evangelism or passing out tracts just doesn't cut it most of the time. People respond to the message of the Gospel when it connects with a need in their lives. To be successful in reaching them, we must tailor the good news to each individual. We will reach our non-Christian friends only by discovering their interests, bearing their burdens, and living authentic Christian lives before them.

If you attend a public school, you are most likely surrounded by non-Christians every day. The key is to find ways to reach out to others and begin building those bridges of love. Try these things for starters:

- *Let people know you are a Christian in a non-threatening way.*

Wear it proudly on your t-shirts and jewelry. Let is blast out of your MP3 player. Publicly pray for your meals, and enthusiastically share the Christian perspective during classroom discussions.

- *Reach out at every opportunity.*

When people tell you about their problems, don't be afraid to pull out your prayer journal and write down their requests. When they ask what you're doing say, "This is important to you. I wanted to make sure that I remember to pray for you and your situation."

If you attend a Christian school or are home schooled, you will have to work a little harder to regularly interact with non-Christians, but you can be just as effective. Here are some ideas to get you started:

- *Join a club or organization.*

The local YMCA, Boys and Girls Club, or Scout programs are great places to start. You might also want to consider signing up for special instruction classes, such as martial arts, theatre, dance, or sports. Remember, these are simply opportunities to interact with "sinners," so don't worry if the idea doesn't seem incredibly cool or adventurous. You aren't doing this for you.

- *Take advantage of your public school friends from church.*

Chances are, they will have plenty of opportunities to introduce you to non-Christians. Go to their ball games, hang out together, etc. You'll be surprised at how many people you meet by simply hanging out. And as was suggested earlier, always be ready with a prayer journal. Remember, people don't care how much you know until they know how much you care.

Many of these suggestions (and many more like them) will place us uncomfortably close to people who do not yet have a relationship with Christ, but we must not allow radical differences to prevent us from connecting with them in their confusion and pain. They are simply sinners in need of a savior. Keep this in mind and it will be easier to be patient with their sinful behaviors as you learn to love them with the love of God in Christ. Doing evangelism from a distance—leaving tracts in public restrooms, for example, or witnessing by e-mail—may feel better, but the reward of seeing redeemed lives is well worth the risk.

Reforming Your Heart

"Though I am free and belong to no man, I make myself a slave to everyone, to win as many as possible. To the Jews I became like a Jew, to win the Jews. To those under the law I became like one under the law (though I myself am not under the law), so as to win

those under the law. To those not having the law I became like one not having the law (though I am not free from God's law but am under Christ's law), so as to win those not having the law. To the weak I became weak, to win the weak. I have become all things to all men so that by all possible means I might save some. I do all this for the sake of the gospel, that I may share in its blessings" (1 Corinthians 9:19–23, NIV).

What do you think Paul meant by this? Most of us have a built-in "phony alarm" that goes off when we know that people aren't being genuine. Do you think Paul was suggesting that we not be real with people?

Reforming Your Mind

Reflect: *Is it possible to be "all things to all men" and still be true to who you are? Why?*

Relate: *The best way that I've found to reach out to others is (share at least one example) .*

Reforming Your Actions

Go out and buy (or sit down and make) a simple prayer journal that will fit in your pocket. Keep it and a pen or pencil with you at all times. Get into the habit of using it every time you pray.

ðay 46

Do You Feel Their Pain?

Let's face it. Gospel tracts are not the best way to interact with an unsaved friend or neighbor. Drive-by "shoutings" and Gospel muggings will never transform our world. In fact, Gospel bombardment can even be counterproductive because it causes an "us vs. them" mentality. Because of the isolation of the Church and our inability to relate, Christians resort to talking *at* unbelievers rather than talking *with* them.

While sitting in a Mexican restaurant eating dinner with my wife, I could not help overhearing a woman at a table next to us preaching fervently to one of the waitresses. Every time this religious zealot spotted the hapless young lady scurrying by with plates or a tray of beverages, she would call out another Bible verse. To make matters worse, the staff knew very little English apart from the items on the menu.

For a while I was almost embarrassed to be a Christian. What bothered me most was not the message but the manner in which it was presented. As the woman's voice got louder and louder, the conversation became less and less private. You could sense everyone's growing contempt for the Christian and pity for the waitress. But the woman was so excited about her opportunity and about what she was saying that she was unaware of the fact that she looked like an idiot. Needless to say, she didn't do anything to make those customers or workers respect Christians or Christianity.

One of the symptoms of being a tract-throwing recluse is that you have lost much of the ability to communicate naturally with unbelievers. Not only is your speech filled with religious jargon that is bewildering to non-Christians, but also you lose your empathy as a listener. We have become far more comfortable in preaching at sinners, using the language of Jerusalem, rather than ministering to them in the language of Babylon.

The truth is, in many situations we would prefer for people to be quiet so we can deliver our message without interruption. While sharing the Gospel, I have actually had the following thought cross my mind: *Would you mind just being quiet so I can preach?* But why? Why do we sometimes feel this way?

For one, I think we are afraid of people's comments and questions. What if they ask a question that we can't answer?

Another problem is that we assume the "sinner" has little or nothing of value to say on the subject. But this is far from the truth. A person's experiences with God, His Word, and His people are always valid, even if they aren't accurate.

The people all around you are looking for someone to affirm them, to listen to what they have to say, to love them, to show them a way out of their pain. In order to do that, you must understand where they are coming from and learn to speak their language. As one Japanese evangelist stated, "We have twice as many ears as we do mouths, so we should spend twice as much time listening as we do talking."

Reforming Your Heart

"When words are many, sin is not absent, but he who holds his tongue is wise" (Proverbs 10:19, NIV).

"A man of knowledge uses words with restraint, and a man of understanding is even-tempered. Even a fool is thought wise if he keeps silent, and discerning if he holds his tongue" (Proverbs 17:27–28, NIV).

"So then, my beloved brethren, let every man be swift to hear, slow to speak, slow to wrath." (James 1:19).

When talking with non-Christians, do you monopolize the conversation with your "great wisdom," or do you listen closely for the heart underneath the words?

Reforming Your Mind

Reflect: *What's the most powerful thing you've ever heard a non-Christian say to you about life?*

Relate: *Tell about an experience you had with an unbelieving friend in which you actually did a good job of simply listening and "being there" instead of preaching.*

Reforming Your Actions

Go to the library and look for a book that teaches you how to be a better listener. Consider taking a course on crisis counseling in order to learn how to better relate to people who are hurting.

ðay 47

Reaching Across the Cultural Aisle

When it comes to doing evangelism in a foreign culture, we can learn a lot from the life of Daniel and his friends. These history-makers received a three-year crash course in the language and literature of Babylon...and they graduated at the very top of their class!

So, how well do you understand the world you live in?

For example, you already know what clothes to wear and how to fix your hair. You probably know what movies are hot, what music is getting *way* too much air time, and which shows are part of the *real* "must-see TV" (not the ones TV execs think are must-see). But does that mean that you really *know* your culture? Not really.

All those things are good, but any dummy can figure those things out simply by being alive and paying attention once in a while. To know your culture, to understand the people you are trying to reach, you have to study. I know, I know...that's a horrible and repugnant thing to say. I'll try not to use the "s" word again. But you can't understand unless you put that brain of yours to work for something other than clever pick-up lines and sharp comebacks. Here are a few things to think about.

The Power of Music

You know what the hottest song is, but do you know how and why it was written? More important, do you know why so many people love it (and trust me, it is *not* simply because it has a funky beat and you can dance to it). Music is powerful in an almost supernatural kind of way. And, for reasons unknown to man, songs have a way of connecting with people way down deep, underneath the surface. When you can start identifying those things, *then* you can say you truly understand your culture. For example, why were patriotic songs suddenly popular again after 9/11? It wasn't the music…it was the message. The hearts of people across America were crying out in pain and in desperation, "God Bless America, land that I love!"

The Power of Fads

There is a world of inexpensive, highly interactive personal knowledge to be gained simply by observing those who live, work and play near you. What's in right now? What's out? What is it that everybody's doing, whether they should be or not? More important, *why* is this particular fad catching on? The answers may be some deep need or they may be really superficial. For example, there may be a fad among girls at school to wear colored pony-tails. And the only "why" behind this fad may be because Suzy Socialite is doing it. But that is still a reason—everybody wants to be like Suzy. Now ask why. What is it about Suzy that people like so much? There may be a dozen reasons, but they probably aren't reasons you've thought about for the purpose of understanding.

We could talk for days about learning to ask *why* in order to gain a clear understanding of what makes people tick. But the bottom line is that without this understanding, you will never be very effective at connecting with people and helping them to find the answers to their deepest questions.

Reforming Your Heart

Read Hebrews chapter 11, about the "Heroes of Faith." The writer of Hebrews goes to great lengths to tell about the things these people did that were extraordinary, even a little on the insane side at times! Notice that the author doesn't leave you hanging by simply telling you what they did, but he explains why they did what they did. Knowing what drives people to do things that at times seem stupid or illogical is what it takes to have a true understanding…the kind of understanding that will enable you to speak truth into their lives in a way that they will gladly hear you.

Reforming Your Mind

Reflect: *What's your favorite song? TV show? movie? Now tell why...and don't wimp out. Think it through.*

Relate: *Here are my favorites (song, TV show, and movie) and here's why...*

Reforming Your Actions

Find a non-Christian today and ask him what is his favorite movie. Ask enough questions to gain a good understanding of why he really liked that movie better than most others. Use that information as a way of learning to relate to and pray for this person.

ðay 48

Prototype Evangelist

The apostle Paul is the premier example of cross-cultural evangelism. One of the clearest examples of the skill with which he crossed cultural barriers was his interaction with the philosophers on Mars Hill.

Paul had developed a habit of finding the local synagogues of whatever town he was in. There he reasoned with the Jewish and Gentile seekers who frequented the synagogue. Before long he was a regular at the open-air market, which was not only a place to buy and sell, but also the real nerve center of the city. At the time, Paul was in Athens waiting for his traveling partners. While he waited, he did a little window shopping, observing all the temples and idols in the city. The Bible says that, upon seeing the massive amounts of idols, "his spirit was provoked within him" (Acts 17:16). So he began talking with the philosophers about a better way. The philosophers were fascinated by Paul's "new teaching" and wanted to hear more.

Then Paul stood in the midst of the Areopagus and said, "Men of Athens, I perceive that in all things you are very religious; for as I was passing through and considering the objects of your worship, I even found an altar with this inscription: TO THE UNKNOWN GOD. Therefore, the One whom you worship without knowing, Him I proclaim to you: God, who made the world and everything in it, since He is Lord of heaven and earth, does not dwell in temples made with hands. Nor is He worshiped with men's hands, as though He needed anything, since He gives to all life, breath, and all things.

"And He has made from one blood every nation of men to dwell on all the face of the earth, and has determined their preappointed times, and the boundaries of their dwellings, so that they should seek the Lord, in the hope that they might grope for Him and find

Him, though He is not far from each one of us; for in Him we live and move and have our being, as also some of your own poets have said, 'For we also are His offspring'" (Acts 17:22–28).

When Paul, a master at cross-cultural communication, was around Jews, he spoke as an expert in the law of Moses and traditions of the elders. When in the presence of the Greeks, he quoted their poets and communicated as one of their own philosophers. What he said of himself was true: "I have become all things to all men, that I might by all means save some" *(1 Corinthians 9:22).*

Paul did not compromise his spiritual values for the sake of cultural relevance. Not on your life. He was open and aggressive in his message, wanting to make it crystal clear that he was "preaching the good news about Jesus and the resurrection" (v.18). Neither can we afford to compromise the message of Christ in order to be seen as relevant by society. Like Paul, postmodern missionaries have to understand where to draw the line between relating and compromise. After all, what people need is not more of what they already have. What they need is what is absent in their lives—the truth that God so loved *us* that He gave His only begotten Son to die in our place!

Reforming Your Heart

"Now the tax collectors and 'sinners' were all gathering around to hear him. But the Pharisees and the teachers of the law muttered, "This man welcomes sinners and eats with them" (Luke 15:1–2, NIV).

Read the rest of Luke 15. Notice the parables that Jesus uses to describe the proper attitude towards sinners. If you were asked to give a five-minute devotion explaining this chapter and you could only talk about how Jesus seems to "feel" about sinners, what would you say? Now describe what Jesus seems to be saying about how we should act toward sinners.

Reforming Your Mind

Reflect: *When you see the kinds of things that your friends are doing, is your "spirit provoked"? What do you think this really means?*

Relate: *There have been many times where I wanted to share with someone about Christ, but I didn't know what or how to say it. For example...*

Reforming Your Actions

The best way to learn to share your faith is by...well, sharing your faith! But that's also the hardest way. Try role-playing with your accountability partner. It isn't quite the same as actually sharing your faith, but it's a good first step.

ðay 49

Discovering Common Ground

Often new converts can be the best soulwinners of all. Why? Because they can relate to the rest of the "natives." They know where the unsaved and unchurched hang out, what they think, and how they feel about professional Christians. They also know the arguments against the Christian faith.

Discovering common ground requires more than simply running through the familiar list of socially acceptable questions: "What's your name? Where are you from? What do you do for a living?" We need to find common interests. Our quest may start with discussing a recent movie or best-selling novel. Find the common ground, then be patient.

After finding the thinnest thread of commonality, many are tempted to charge into a confrontation about the other person's relationship with God. But if you do, you are communicating that you really did not care that much about the previous conversation. All you wanted to do was get an opportunity to pounce on your unsuspecting prey.

Which poses a good question. Let me ask it as a reminder: Do you really care about your neighbor or schoolmate as a person, or do you primarily care about preaching to him or her? Jesus related to people and was well received by them—not because He had a well-rehearsed sales pitch, but because He really loved them for who they were, right where they were.

Think about Paul's example. He didn't ask a few pleasant questions and then "go for the jugular." Instead, Paul began with what was commonly accepted, and progressed logically, step by step, to Jesus Christ who rose from the dead. He was patient. He took his time with people. He showed genuine concern for and interest in their ideas and lives. Besides, quoting a Bible verse to prove something settles nothing. If your friend does not accept the Bible as a source of authority, make your point another way.

Using the Power of Shared Beliefs

Your ultimate intention is to reveal the truth that is yet unknown to this person. To do that, it's often best to start out by confirming what he or she already believes to be true. In other words, show some respect for where he is in his own journey of faith. He may still be light years away from the truth, but if you start out by saying (or implying) that every aspect of his belief system is simply wrong while every aspect of yours is unquestionably true, there is a good possibility you will run into some resistance.

It is important to remember that all truth is God's truth, even if it is not religious truth. So look for things that he already believes that you can agree with him about. Then confirm truth, but do it carefully. When you do this, you will give him a reason to trust your motives as pure and genuine.

Reforming Your Heart

"On one occasion an expert in the law stood up to test Jesus. 'Teacher,' he asked, 'what must I do to inherit eternal life?'

"'What is written in the Law?' he replied. 'How do you read it?'

"'He answered: 'Love the Lord your God with all your heart and with all your soul and with all your strength and with all your mind' ; and, 'Love your neighbor as yourself.'"

"'You have answered correctly,'" Jesus replied. 'Do this and you will live'" (Luke 10:25–28, NIV).

Notice that Jesus not only asked this man for his opinion, but he also applauded the man for speaking the truth instead of pointing out what He probably already knew—this man was a sinner in need of a savior.

Reforming Your Mind

Reflect: *When talking with non-Christians, do you find it easy or difficult to encourage them when they speak the truth? Why?*

Relate: *Think about a friend at school who is part of a non-Christian religion. What do you admire most about this person? Why?*

Reforming Your Actions

Can you think of a friend at school who has bought into the lies of Islam, Hinduism or Buddhism? If so, determine to learn a little about the basic beliefs of their religion so that when you talk with them, you can applaud any untainted truth while at the same time pointing them toward the perfect truth of Jesus Christ.

ðay 50

To Babylon and Back

Paul is a prime example of someone who could reach across a great divide and influence a culture. He knew the language, he understood the culture, he had a good grip on what most of the people believed, and he was able to figure out where to be flexible and where to take a bold, uncompromising stand for truth.

Most people of foreign cultures are honored when they meet a person who has taken the time to learn their language and customs. Usually they are eager to talk. For Daniel and his friends it was a matter of survival. For us it is a matter of choice and obedience to the Great Commission.

For the past forty-nine days we've taken a long hard look at what it means to reach our generation. Maybe you're feeling pumped right now—maybe you're feeling overwhelmed. But even if you are feeling like the job is too complicated, be encouraged. Learning the language of Babylon is not as complicated as it seems. Over time our ability to talk with nonbelievers in a natural way may be more a reflection of our genuine respect and consideration than any other thing we've talked about thus far. Not only do we need to love people with the love of Christ, but we have to show them courtesy, even when they have wrong ideas, even when they are in bondage to sin, even when they persecute us. We cannot afford to become so passionate about being right that we forget to be kind.

As the earthly representatives of the Kingdom of God in this world, why would we not seek to express the presence, character and power of the King in every area of life? How did Jesus respond when confronted with these very issues in His generation? He reached out to Samaritans, Gentiles, children, harlots, tax collectors, legalistic Pharisees, insane demoniacs, rich young rulers, untouchable lepers, Roman centurions, and fishermen. He ministered in synagogues, on the hillside, in the Temple, at weddings, in home groups, and before the chief representative of Rome. Then He sent His own representatives out to every tribe, tongue, people group, and nation.

From what area of life did He exclude Himself? When Jesus looked at the world, what aspect of Jewish or Roman culture did He consider to be outside the realm of His Lordship and apart from those things that are to be put under His feet?

Nada. Zip. Zilch. He was, is, and always will be King of kings, Lord over all.

Learning the language of Babylon is like building an expansion bridge to connect with a very different world. Making contact is only the first step. In order to touch a person's heart, you have to communicate eternal truth with love and compassion. More important, to be like Christ is to identify with and be numbered among the transgressors, yet without sin. That was the challenge to Daniel in Babylon, to Jesus in Judea, to Terry Crist in a postmodern community—and to you, wherever you live.

Will you accept the challenge?

Reforming Your Heart

"For God so loved the world that he gave his one and only Son, that whoever believes in him shall not perish but have eternal life. For God did not send his Son into the world to condemn the world, but to save the world through him. Whoever believes in him is not condemned, but whoever does not believe stands condemned already because he has not believed in the name of God's one and only Son. This is the verdict: Light has come into the world, but men loved darkness instead of light because their deeds were evil. Everyone who does evil hates the light, and will not come into the light for fear that his deeds will be exposed. But whoever lives by the truth comes into the light, so that it may be seen plainly that what he has done has been done through God" (John 3:16–21, NIV).

Do you really understand the message of John? It is not a message of condemnation or even of justice. It is a message of love and grace and mercy. God so loves…can you afford to do any less?

Reforming Your Mind

Reflect: *Name one person in your life to whom you have the hardest time showing genuine love, care, and respect. Why?.*

Relate: *The one person in my life that I have the hardest time showing genuine love, care and respect for is _____ because _____.*

Reforming Your Actions

Pray fervently with your accountability partner for the individuals you each just identified. Do this every single day for the next thirty days. Watch your person as closely as you can during this time of intercession. Learn to speak his language. Then ask God to give you a heart of mercy and compassion for him and to open up a door for you to share the love of God with him (or her).

Notes

Day 3
1. *Eerdmans' Handbook to Christianity in America* (Grand Rapids: Eerdmans, 1983), p.321.
2. Cited in Gene Edward Veith Jr., *Postmodern Times: a Christian Guide to Contemporary Thought and Culture* (Wheaton, Ill.: Crossway, 1994), pp.44-46

Day 21
1. A. W. Tozer, *The Dwelling Place of God* (Harrisburg, Pa.: Christian Publications, 1966), p. 53.

Day 26
1. *The Atlanta Journal-Constitution*, Thursday, August 24, 1989. *The Dekalb News*, Sunday Edition, August, 9, 1989.
2. Paul Tillich, *The Irrelevance and Relevance of the Christian Message* (Cleveland,: Pilgrim's Press, 1996), p. 13.
3. Ibid.

Day 27
1. Abraham Kyper, *A Centennial Reader,* ed. James D. Bratt (Grand Rapids: Eerdmans, 1998), p. 461.

Day 32
1. Stanley Jones, *The Unshakeable Kingdom and the Unchanging Person* (Nashville: Abingdon, 1972), p. 19.

Day 33

    1. Vine's Complete Expository Dictionary of Biblical Words (Nashville: Thomas Nelson, 1985), s.v. "blessed."

Day 38

    1. Bob Beckett, *Commitment to Conquer* (Grand Rapids: Chosen Books, 1997), p. 65.

Terry M. Crist
SpiritBuilder Resources & Seminars
P. O. Box 14553
Scottsdale, AZ 85267

480.661.9209
www.terrycrist.com
www.citichurch.com

Printed in the United States
33709LVS00003B/164